WHITETAIL SPRING

WHITETAIL SPRING

SEASONS OF THE WHITETAIL
BOOK THREE

Text by John J. Ozoga

WILLOW CREEK PRESS
Minocqua, Wisconsin

PHOTOGRAPHY:

Jeanne Drake, pp. 2, 68, 113, 116, 131.

Bill Lea, pp. 5, 8, 10, 21, 27, 32, 48, 54, 55, 60, 62, 64, 65, 71, 74, 80, 83, 85, 86, 93, 109, 124, 140, 144.

Maslowski Wildlife Productions, pp. 11, 30, 66, 128.

Len Rue, Jr., pp. 12, 17, 26, 88, 90, 95, 99–108, 114, 121.

Charles J. Alsheimer, pp. 15, 22, 28, 44, 47, 61, 63, 70, 72, 75, 79, 82, 126.

Bill Marchel, pp. 16, 25, 42, 53, 56, 130, 132.

Henry F. Zeman, pp. 18, 20, 41, 69, 116, 117.

Donald M. Jones, pp. 24, 38, 58, 87, 129.

Richard P. Smith, pp. 29, 36, 51, 76, 91, 97, 110, 112, 122, 134.

Al Cornell, pp. 33, 35, 52, 125, 135.

Ozoga, Janice, p. 40.

Ozoga, Holly, p. 78.

Greg Gersbach, p. 136.

Michael H. Francis, pp. 67, 137.

Gary L. Alt, p. 138.

Designed by Patricia Bickner Linder

Published by WILLOW CREEK PRESS, P.O. Box 147, Minocqua, WI 54548

For information on other Willow Creek titles, write or call 1-800-850-WILD.

Library of Congress Cataloging-in-Publication Data

Ozoga, John J.
     Whitetail spring / text by John J. Ozoga.
          p.   cm.   — (Seasons of the whitetail ; bk. 3)
     Includes bibliographical references (p. 141).
     ISBN 1-57223-039-8 (hc : alk. paper)
     1. White-tailed deer. 2. Spring.   I. Title. II. Series: Ozoga,
John J. Seasons of the whitetail ; bk. 3.
     QL737.U550965   1996
     599.73'57—dc20
                                                    96-6030
                                                      CIP

Printed in Canada.

ACKNOWLEDGEMENTS

Needless to say, this series of books — Seasons of the Whitetail — has provided me a very special opportunity to put together many pieces of the whitetail puzzle for the benefit of those who share my deep concern for this amazing species. And, I'm indebted to many, including those mentioned in *Whitetail Autumn* and *Whitetail Winter*, books one and two, for their help.

Although I'd studied white-tailed deer since about 1960, I didn't put much of the research findings into popular form until the mid-1980s, and then only after considerable coaxing by my wife, Janice. If not for her foresight and encouragement, none of these books would have come to be.

Many people in the publishing business helped and encouraged me along the way, but Chuck and Tom Petrie were by far the most influential. I don't know anyone who writes easily and well — it's pure hard work — but the Petries have made my job easier, and, quite frankly, enjoyable. I'd like to extend a special thanks to Chuck and Tom, and to the rest of the staff at Willow Creek Press; their expertise shows in the quality of these pages.

This is a "coffee table" book, whatever precisely that may be; I presume that the text must be well illustrated to qualify. Be that as it may, the pictures herein tell the story most vividly. By all means, readers, look closely at the front portion of this book and the names of photographers who helped me relate to you the story of *Whitetail Spring*. These people are among the best in the business.

My good friend Ed Langenau kindly provided the foreword to this book, for which I'm very grateful. Ed is an extremely talented individual. He specialized in human dimensions research, primarily as it relates to deer management, with the Michigan Department of Natural Resources before becoming the state's big game specialist. Among other things, he is now responsible for coordinating a deer management program that ranks near the top in the nation for deer harvest and hunter recreation.

I don't ever recall seeing the readership acknowledged in a book, but I will. The response I've received from hunters and nonhunters to books one and two in this series and the sincere interest shown for the well-being of whitetails has been most gratifying. Knowing that readers appreciate my efforts and learn from the material I present is more important to me than I can express. Thanks to all of you, from the bottom of my heart.

DEDICATION

To John, Holly, Mark, and Keith. How very
dull life would have been without you.

CONTENTS

FOREWORD

Social research has shown that Americans appreciate deer more than any other wild species. The domesticated horse is the only animal that is more popular.

The intense public interest in deer may relate to the historical role this animal played in the development of our country. Native Americans, trappers, and pioneers depended on deer for their survival. Another reason for our attraction to deer may reflect an instinctive fascination with the most cunning of all prey species. Individuals who have hunted moose, elk, sheep, and other big game species often report that the white-tailed deer is the most challenging to seek. Deer also evoke strong emotions in people. Bucks provoke imagery of strength and majesty; does, beauty and grace; and fawns, innocence and maternal protection. Many people who live in urbanized environments perceive the white-tailed deer as a symbol of wilderness. Deer remind us of a basic connection between people and the land.

Five million whitetail fawns are born in the United States alone each year. The young animals are symbolic of our rich wildlife heritage and a reminder of our responsibility to shepherd their habitat.

The white-tailed deer series from Willow Creek Press especially satisfies this need for a connection with nature. The collection of photographs in these books offers potent images to excite our imagination. The text blends these visual sensations to create a coherent understanding of deer. As a result, the reader gains a deeper appreciation for the biology and sociology of this mystical species.

The author of this series, John Ozoga, is a master wordsmith. His writing depicts our love for deer. John writes to many different individuals — hunters, wildlife viewers, artists, landowners, and ecologists. His words flow vividly to portray the complex life of whitetails in a manner that is easily understood.

Not only is John an outstanding writer, but he also has a thorough knowledge of his subject. He spent three decades as a wildlife research biologist with the Michigan Department of Natural Resources Wildlife Division. He conducted pioneering studies on the social behavior of whitetails. The results of his research have been published in professional journals such as the *Journal of Wildlife Management* and *Journal of Mammalogy*.

John's research has been a careful blend of experimental science and field observation. His contributions to the scientific literature on white-tailed deer have become classic studies that have built a sound foundation for management and future research.

Whitetail Spring shows us the capacity deer have for recovery after the stress of winter weather and food shortages. The beginning of antler development in bucks drives them to search for vegetation with high mineral composition. Fetal growth occurs rapidly with the rejuvenation of buds, leaves, and forest grasses that provide food for pregnant does. All of these processes are directed to the production and care of a new generation of deer.

Each year, more than five million whitetail deer are born throughout the United States. Those fawns help us realize that humans have a moral responsibility to be good stewards of the earth. They also remind us that life is a cycle of birth, growth, reproduction, maturity, and death.

— *Ed Langenau, Big Game Specialist*
Michigan Department of Natural Resources

The whitetails' annual cycle culminates in spring with the appearance of a new generation of deer. Each new fawn carries with it adaptive genetic material shaped by thousands of years of selective pressures.

INTRODUCTION

I've never lived in the southern United States, so I really can't surmise how southerners perceive the spring season. In the North, however, spring is a fascinating and mentally uplifting time of the year — a time of recovery and rebirth that touches virtually every living thing. And despite its initially capricious nature, once it begins in earnest, spring is normally a bountiful time of year for bedraggled white-tailed deer. It is then that they return to their favored summering grounds, where they labor to recover from the hardships of the stressful winter season.

The dictionary tells us that "spring" means to move upward, forward, or come forth suddenly. As a season, it is that time "occurring between winter and summer, during which the weather becomes warmer and plants revive, extending in the Northern Hemisphere from the vernal equinox to the summer solstice and popularly considered to comprise March, April, and May."

By late spring, bucks that survived the previous winter will already be growing antlers in preparation for the coming autumn rut. Antler size, among other factors, will determine which males will attain breeding rights in autumn.

In the midwestern and northeastern parts of their range in the United States, whitetails' first glimpses of spring coincide with the seasonal gathering of sap and manufacture of maple syrup.

March and April spring? For northern whitetails? Popular indeed! In the South, and even in the lower Midwest, spring sometimes does, in fact, burst forth suddenly — often in March. But northward, where frigid temperatures and snow cover may linger, spring tends to be an unpredictable and rather teasing sort of season.

In the Upper Great Lakes region, the Northeast, and in the Northern Plains states, brief periods of unseasonable warmth during early spring are frequently interrupted with untimely cold, blizzardlike weather. Sub-zero temperatures are not uncommon in March, and a foot or more of wet, heavy snow — sometimes even in May — can suddenly blanket a landscape otherwise struggling to revive with new green growth.

Therefore, while popularly referred to as spring, during some years on northern deer range, the month of March and oftentimes most of April might more appropriately be labeled winter. And when contemplating seasons of the whitetail, I'm also inclined to refer to early June as late spring.

For northern whitetails in particular, spring signals survival. It is, of course, a decisive season for them because it is during that time of year that the next generation is born. Also, any given spring period might embrace some of the most stressful, as well as the most favorable, environmental conditions the species is likely to experience throughout the year. Despite spring's dubious demeanor, however, the adaptable whitetail possesses certain innate defenses and has evolved strategies to cope with the unpleasant environmental conditions that sometimes arise.

Fortunately, the whitetail's reproductive rhythm is regulated by photoperiod and not by some other cue, such as temperature, which oscillates more wildly and follows a less predictable seasonal cycle. Whitetails are "short-day breeders," in that fewer hours of daylight during autumn cause hormonal changes responsible for their breeding behavior. In the North, the whitetail's breeding window is relatively narrow and keyed to ensure that the vast majority of fawns are born on schedule in spring when weather and vegetative conditions are most favorable for survival.

Due to natural selection, therefore, does seldom give birth to vulnerable fawns during the treacherous late winter to early spring period. Nor do many does on northern range err by giving birth during mid-summer, as the young would not mature sufficiently to survive their first winter. Understandably, the whitetail's fawning season can be much more protracted in the South, where climatic factors are less stressful.

In spring, before the fawns are born, there will be far

In spring, as temperatures rise and days begin to lengthen, whitetails will shed their heavy winter coats for their sleek red pelage of spring and summer. During the molting period, however, the animals appear scruffy and unkempt.

fewer deer in any given population compared to the peak numbers that occurred the previous autumn. This is largely due to their autumn ranks being thinned by human hunters. In the North, too, the grim months of winter will have removed large numbers of small, weak, injured, and old-age animals via malnutrition and predation, leaving primarily the strongest and hardiest stock.

Following severe winters, therefore, surviving whitetails will be those that possess special adaptive traits — inherited characteristics that enhance the species' survival prospects under the prevailing environmental constraints where they live. These deer, the products of natural selection, will be the ones best suited to live in their locale. And they, the survivors, will be the ones that pass on their genetic material and contribute most significantly to the hardiness of future generations.

Granted, winter's grim reaper will cull the sick, lame, and other unfit animals from the herd. Come spring, however, after having endured cold temperatures, ice, snow, and driving winds for several months and having subsisted upon meager amounts of poor-quality food, even the survivors will appear scruffy, gaunt, and infirm.

Following a tough winter, many of those whitetails that venture from their winter quarters will be literally drained of their energy stores, and they'll be strikingly thin. Their ribs show conspicuously, and their hip bones protrude through their thick, highly insulative, but tattered and worn winter coats.

By winter's end, whitetails will begin to molt. Their winter hair will be coarse, brittle, and loose; it falls out easily when the animals shake themselves. Since molting tends to commence on the animal's neck, skinny-necked, puffy-faced individuals soon acquire a pathetic ostrichlike appearance.

Others, those scarred from fighting, will display huge spots of pinkish skin, likely where the hoof of another deer struck while the two debated which animal would consume some choice morsel of food. Before long, however, the bare spots darken and become the first places where red summer hair appears. By late spring, some whitetails will be sleek and trim in their new summer coats. Meanwhile, though, during early spring, the otherwise elegant, graceful, and normally beautiful whitetail will appear pitifully shabby and unkempt.

In addition to their outward, physical appearance, whitetails experience considerable changes during late winter and early spring. Commencing about mid-March, in response to the lengthening of daylight hours (photoperiod), they change immensely in basic physiological processes and general behavior. Their metabolism rises and, compared to the ultraconservative lifestyle they demonstrate in winter, they become much more active. Thereafter, given the opportunity, their food intake rates rise sharply to meet their increasing metabolic demands.

All deer, regardless of sex or age, seem to share a common obsession in spring: finding and consuming as much nutritious food as possible. They do so to replace body tissues depleted during the previous rut and stressful months of winter. It is in spring, too, that immature animals resume growing, and bucks start growing a new set of antlers. Pregnant does, then in their final trimester of pregnancy, carry rapidly enlarging fetuses that sap each mother's scant energy reserves. A gravid doe, then, will glean major benefits from whatever nutritious food she can consume. Hence, in spring, access to copious amounts of nutritious forage in the form of succulent new herbaceous growth high in protein, energy, and essential minerals and vitamins is exceedingly important for all deer, even the unborn.

The month of May, before fawns are born and when woodlands and meadows begin to flush with colorful, ephemeral flora, represents one of the whitetail's more sociable times of the year. This is a good time for deer because nutritious food abounds almost everywhere. This is when whitetails intermingle peaceably, gorge on the succulent new growth, and seldom assert social rank or bicker over available food and cover resources.

But all that will change, and the species will enter a brief but socially turbulent period during the fawning season. Does heavy with young are normally indulgent and fairly docile creatures. However, once their young are born, they become aggressive mothers; they will viciously attack any other deer straying into their jealously guarded fawning grounds, where their newborn lay in hiding. It's a socially disruptive period when nursing does greatly influence, if not dictate, deer distribution and thereby play a key role in the nutritional well-being of other deer within the herd.

Shortly after birth, a fawn will be kept in seclusion in a fawning area that is exclusively the domain of its mother. Any other deer straying into the site will be aggressively repelled by the protective doe.

Yearling does remain in the matriarchal area with older, mature females, and at times may feed in association with members of their doe clan. All females that have given birth, however, will retreat from the gathering several times per day to attend their secluded young.

The doe who gave birth to these day-old twin fawns will soon move them to separate hiding areas, to improve one fawn's chance of survival in the event a predator discovers the other one.

The strength of the bond established between a doe and her fawn will have profound influences on the fawn's survival and, later, its social status within the herd.

Until the does' secretive and pugnacious attitude subsides, other deer must adjust their social habits and general activities accordingly. It is at this time of year, when the fawns are born, that segregation of the sexes becomes pronounced. Each animal then must jockey to secure favorable space, food, and cover resources as best it can.

It's only been recently that researchers have begun to understand the intricate details of the whitetails' behavior during this brief but intriguing time of year. And although those of us close to the subject still debate the behavioral, ecological, and evolutionary relationships involved, it is now readily apparent that the spring season is a behaviorally dynamic and nutritionally important period for whitetails.

What transpires during whitetail spring — that precarious time between the vernal equinox and the summer solstice — will determine whether the next generation of whitetails flourishes or fails.

Spring ushers forth a plethora of new growth, nutritious food vital to winter-stressed pregnant whitetails, to hungry yearlings, and to bucks whose energy stores became depleted months previously, during the fall rut.

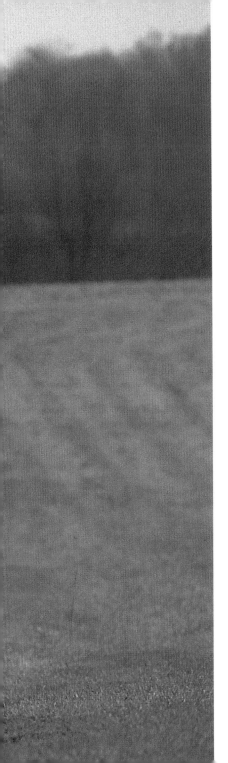

SOCIAL BEHAVIOR

An animal's social habits and most other facets of its behavior are inherited and adapted to the environment in which it lives. The whitetail's behavioral traits, then, are no less genetically linked and are as critical to the species' healthful existence as are its physical and physiological capabilities. And because the hardy whitetail has adapted to survive in a wide array of landscapes, ranging from Canada to South America, whitetail subspecies tend to appear physically and behave somewhat differently across the species' vast geographical range.

In white-tailed deer, the adult sexes live separately during much of the year, as do mule deer, red deer, elk, moose, bighorn sheep, and other ungulates. Scientists refer to this social and spatial separation as "sexual segregation" or "niche separation" of the sexes.

When winter's snow and ice dissipate, whitetails gather anywhere an abundance of new growth may appear. Most of the groupings are of socially compatible and, in the case of does, related animals.

Where choice patches of food are found, even related does may become covetous of feeding rights and show aggression toward one another. When low level aggressive displays by a dominant female fail to deter another doe, a brief but physical "flailing" encounter may ensue.

Based on intensive behavioral investigations at southern Michigan's George Reserve, Dale McCullough and his co-workers concluded that because of gender differences in use of space, food, and cover, bucks and does do not compete for the necessities of life on a year-round basis.

Sex segregation is especially pronounced among whitetails in late spring, during the fawning season, when does with newborn seek seclusion and become extremely aggressive toward intruders of their own species. Nursing does then defend their traditional fawning grounds, areas that provide adequate hiding cover for the newborn and are best suited for rearing fawns. In contrast, adult bucks band together in small groups and seek areas where nutrition is superb, which allows for maximum body growth to attain a high dominance rank and improved breeding success.

In northern and eastern North America, most whitetails live in deciduous or coniferous forest cover.

However, in the western and southwestern parts of the country, the species can be found in predominantly open areas, such as broad plains and savanna habitat. But even where they occupy open areas, whitetails require a certain amount of protective cover, in the form of brush or trees, where they can rest and hide from predators. Hiding cover is especially important for newborn fawns threatened by predators, and vigilant mothers also often prefer to remain hidden. However, although farm fields and forest openings add valuable diversity to deer habitat, and some openness is an important component of good quality deer habitat, nowhere in its vast range is the whitetail strictly an open plains animal.

Socially speaking, when compared to other, more gregarious ungulates, especially plains dwellers such as bison and antelope, the white-tailed deer is more of a loner. It is regarded as an individualistic or solitary species because it generally lives alone or in small groups.

Seasonal segregation of the sexes in whitetails is most evident after spring breakup when does leave wintering areas to return to their traditional fawn-rearing territories.

This doesn't mean that it is antisocial. At some times of the year, and especially in certain environments, whitetails periodically gather in large, mixed groups of bucks, does, and fawns.

Throughout their range, large groups of whitetails are especially evident during the early autumn period, and also during winter and early spring on northern range. In autumn, deer often gather in farm fields, in food plots planted specifically for them, or in natural openings. Primarily, these gatherings are the result of deer responding to concentrations of choice herbaceous forage. But sometimes such autumn gatherings of deer seem to form immediately prior to the breeding season and strictly for communicative, social purposes.

In many northern regions, due to cold weather, deep snow, and the threat of predators, deer are literally forced to vacate much of their summer range. Many whitetails then migrate as much as 50 miles, or farther in some instances, and sometimes congregate in great numbers in conifer habitat that offers them favorable shelter. In other words, winter aggregations of deer tend to form out of necessity, as a special adaptation for survival during the harsh winter season.

SPRING AGGREGATIONS

In spring, open areas are the first places where snow melts and new herbaceous growth appears. Open, south-facing slopes will be free of snow several weeks before snow melts beneath dense conifers where deer seek protection during the cold, snowy months of winter. When the snowpack begins to rot beneath the dense conifers, making travel there especially hazardous, open areas will provide deer easy travel conditions. In addition, the sun's rays soon warm the earth and stimulate the growth of herbaceous plants, in the form of grasses and various forbs, some of which remain green beneath the snow. The succulent herbs provide important nutritious forage that supplements the whitetail's otherwise meager winter diet of coarse, woody browse. Hence, open areas adjacent to winter deer "yarding" areas are especially important to whitetails during the early spring period.

In spring, large aggregations of deer in openings along the periphery of winter yarding areas may outwardly appear as disorganized herds. Actually, such gatherings will consist of discrete matriarchal and fraternal groups — socially bonded does and their young, and groups of compatible mature bucks, respectively. Group members share certain range during the snow-free months, interact frequently, and band together in protective cover during winter.

Following a tough winter, however, deer deaths due to malnutrition and predation may leave some individuals

Open areas adjacent to winter deer "yards" provide some of the first new grasses and forbs of the season. Groups of whitetails are commonly seen in these openings in early spring.

Signs of aggressiveness in spring, especially following snowmelt, are
routine in deer society and help maintain order within the dominance
hierarchy of the various clans.

without social allies. Young deer without stronger adult companions may then find themselves particularly handicapped when competing for choice feeding locations.

When in crowded situations, which commonly occur briefly on northern deer range during spring break-up, whitetails naturally appear edgy and somewhat cantankerous. This might be expected when members of such an individualistic species are forced into close contact with one another. And while socially bonded individuals periodically engage in rather aggressive interactions, among aggregations of deer in spring, the most serious conflicts will break out between animals that are not socially compatible.

Since deer readily recognize one another, and members of social groups are ranked in a rather strict dominance-hierarchy, low level threat behaviors generally suffice to decide dominance and establish elbowroom when deer congregate at choice feeding spots. Deer normally avoid direct eye contact, as it tends to invite some sort of behavioral response, favorable or otherwise. Therefore, by winter's end, among deer familiar to one another, a mere glance or flick of an ear may suffice as a threatening signal: "Step aside or look out."

Normally, an aggressive encounter between two equally matched, antlerless whitetails follows a rather predictable progression from subtle threat displays to potentially damaging strikes with the forelegs. A typical encounter might start with an "ear-drop" and direct stare, or "hard-look," progress to a feeble foreleg strike, then to a lunge, or rush, sometimes accompanied by a snort, and terminate with both combatants standing on their hind legs and slapping or "flailing" at one another. Depending upon how closely matched the two contestants are, however, a weaker subordinate might turn and run at any point during the contest.

In early spring, when bucks are antlerless, mature does and adult bucks might forgo the subtle preliminaries and suddenly burst into a wild flailing bout. Even an adult doe is no match for a large-antlered buck. However, an older, battle-experienced doe may readily hold her ground, stand on her hind legs, reach as high as she can, and duke it out with an antlerless buck much larger than herself. She'll more than likely lose when combating a healthy prime-aged buck, but occasionally emerges victorious over younger bucks or older ones that are injured or otherwise physically handicapped.

Although large aggregations of deer may form at break-up chiefly in response to concentrated nutritious forage, deer in large groups also find greater safety from predators. When comparing the social behavior of whitetails living in heavily forested northern Michigan

*In the north whitetails migrate, usually in groups, from their winter
range to summer range. These migrations may require from a few
hours to two weeks to accomplish, depending on weather and the
distance between the traditional seasonal ranges.*

to that of whitetails living on Texas grasslands, for example, biologist David Hirth found that groups of deer in both locations were always smallest in dense cover and largest in open areas with no cover. He observed low levels of aggression among deer on the open grasslands and concluded that the formation of large social groups in open areas evolved primarily as an adaptation for predator avoidance.

SPRING MIGRATION

In spring, deer on northern range seem anxious to return to their summer range as soon as temperatures moderate and snow melts. In the Upper Great Lakes region, depending upon the rate and timing of snowmelt, migration may sometimes occur in early March, but during some years will not commence until early May.

In northern Minnesota, researchers Mike Nelson and Dave Mech observed that spring migration onset always occurred after maximum daily temperature shifted from below freezing to consistently above freezing. For unknown reasons, however, some deer delayed migrating until two to three weeks after snowmelt.

Even in Midwest farmlands, some deer migrate long distances to occupy preferred habitat during winter. On the intensively farmed lands of Illinois, for example,

researchers led by Charles Nixon found that about 20 percent of white-tailed deer migrated seasonally. Unlike deer living farther north, however, spring migration of the farmland deer was not governed by temperature or snow depths. Instead, the farmland deer usually did not return to their summer ranges until early April, or not until leaf-out was well advanced and temperatures were well above freezing.

The migrations of deer to their summer ranges in spring tends to be more direct and faster than their fall migrations to winter habitat; the spring movements may vary from only a few hours to as much as two weeks in duration. As is sometimes characteristic of fall migrations, however, whitetails may exhibit several false starts, temporarily returning to the protection of yarding cover when temperatures drop, before finally migrating. Although fast migration sometimes compensates for late departures from deer yards, studies have shown that the farther the distance between winter yards and summer ranges, the longer the duration of migration.

Some deer may migrate to their summer range alone, but most migrate in groups. Related does and their fawns, the latter of which require adult guidance in order to reach distant summer ranges, may occasionally travel in groups of a dozen or more animals. They usually follow a fairly straight course from winter to summer

range, probably the same path they followed during fall migration to wintering cover. Adult bucks more often travel alone or with one or two other socially compatible males; they also tend to wander while migrating. It's not unusual, however, for several different social groups to follow the same migration path for many miles before settling on their individual, traditional summering grounds.

TRADITIONAL RANGE

Adult whitetails develop strong attachment to their

Seasonal ranges and migration paths are traditional among deer clans. Young deer learn their way to winter range and how to return to summer range by following mature, migration-experienced does.

established home ranges. In southern environments a deer may spend its entire lifetime in an area of less than one square mile. But even those deer that live on northern range and migrate long distances seasonally return to a relatively small, familiar home range each spring.

Where a deer lives is determined more by its early social experience, learning, and traditional habits than by some mystical ability to select the best habitat available. According to University of Georgia researchers Larry Marchinton and Karl Miller: "Different generations of whitetails often maintain very similar home ranges even if there are no artificial 'property lines,' such as cliffs or fences, to keep the young deer from using feeding or bedding sites different from those of their mothers. This is particularly true of females and suggests a cultural component. In other words, the traditional home range, and familiarity with it, can be conveyed from one generation to the next."

There are certain advantages for a prey species such as the whitetail to become very familiar with its surroundings. As the Georgia researchers emphasize: "If [a prey species] knows the area well enough, it can obtain the necessities of life — escape from potential causes of death — with great efficiency. The range must be large enough to provide sufficient resources and cover, yet it must be small enough for the animal to know it well."

In spring, especially on northern range, deer tend to explore beyond the boundaries of their home range and sometimes extend their range if conditions permit. Depending upon the environment, certain habitats provide a brief flush of foliage before trees and shrubs attain leaf-out. Given the opportunity, deer seem quick to take advantage of such bountiful forage, even if it means meandering more than they may usually do. It is at this time of year, before fawns are born, that females and their nearly one-year-old offspring intermingle with bucks and other unrelated family groups in their quest for nutritious food. This tendency to explore and range farther than usual, but then return to traditional ground to give birth to fawns, may partly explain why does seem to select fawning areas on the periphery of their home range.

MATRIARCHAL GROUPS

Most female whitetails remain on familiar range and live in a matriarchal social system comprising related individuals. Depending upon environmental conditions, reproductive success, and longevity, such a female social unit may consist of an old doe — the matriarch — and her daughters, granddaughters, great-granddaughters, and even great-great-granddaughters. Members of the clan tend to share a common ancestral range during

much of the year and may band together in groups during the autumn and winter period. When raising fawns, however, each female occupies an exclusive area that she defends, and from which she aggressively drives away all other deer.

Generally, unless she is extremely old, the clan matriarch is the dominant female in the group. She tends to breed and fawn first and controls the most favorable fawn-rearing habitat within the ancestral range. Younger does within the matriarchy, especially those impregnated for the first time, are generally bred after the matriarch

Matriarchal groups often comprise several generations of related does, the oldest of which is usually the most dominant female in the group.

from being closely aligned with a maternally experienced doe when the newborn are threatened by predators. This system of range occupation serves to maintain the matriarch's traditional fawning ground and allows for expansion of the clan's ancestral range during times when food and cover resources are ideal and conducive to population growth.

On the other hand, if older females are removed from the population — via predation, hunting mortality or other causes — voids will occur within the ancestral range. Second-time mothers then probably will not leave their natal range to raise fawns because dispersal to new range is risky and often leads to excessive mortality among the newborn.

Noted scientist Tony Peterle proposed that deer should have developed certain sociobiological traits during their evolution that would enable them to cope with constantly changing food availability and simultaneously control population size and prevent starvation due to overutilization of food sources.

In my view, the whitetails' matriarchal social organization and territorial behavior associated with raising young fawns evolved primarily to *maximize* reproductive success, even in the presence of effective predators. Clearly, the female whitetail social system is one that allows the species to make efficient use of food and cover

has bred; hence they fawn later and may have difficulty finding suitable fawn-rearing habitat when deer density is high or, for some other reason, food and cover resources are limited.

Typically, the matriarch returns each year to her traditional fawning ground to rear her young. Within the matriarch's clan, does fawning for their second time usually shift their fawn-rearing areas about a quarter-mile from their previous birthing location. Young does fawning for the first time will establish exclusive fawning areas adjacent to their mothers, and sometimes benefit

The youngest does in a matriarchal group have least priority when staking out secure fawning areas. When deer densities are high, such does often suffer high fawn mortality when relegated to raising their offspring in areas with inadequate cover.

resources as they become available.

Certainly, naturally occurring fires and those set by primitive man, floods, windstorms, and similar calamities periodically devastated mature forests, set back vegetation succession, and produced patches of ideal habitat for whitetails. The female whitetails' social system permits the species to take quick advantage of abundant food and cover that results from such environmental disasters. It is also a system that allows harmonious occupation of favorable habitat occurring in patches, maximum reproductive success, and rapid population growth when the appropriate circumstances arise.

FRATERNAL GROUPS

Among whitetails, males are the dispersing sex. That is, whereas female whitetails likely remain on, or close to, ancestral range throughout their lifetime and frequently interact with related females, males tend to disperse to new range where they associate with unrelated deer of both sexes. Most males disperse during autumn, when 16 to 17 months old, and achieve social bonds with other, probably unrelated, males during the autumn period. But sometimes they disperse at younger or older age, and during other seasons.

When not in breeding condition, whitetail bucks are reasonably docile and highly sociable creatures. Then they typically live in all-male, or fraternal, groups. In fact, some investigators claim that mature whitetail bucks may achieve closer social bonding in their unrelated fraternal groups than do most mature, related whitetail does in matriarchal clans.

Sexually mature whitetail males are physically repelled by related females. Consequently, young bucks that have attained or are reaching sexual maturity leave, or are driven away by, the female-dominated clan into which they were born. To find breeding opportunities, the young buck leaves the home range of its mother's clan. In his exodus, the young buck seeks affiliation with an unrelated fraternal group. Since a male's breeding opportunities are determined by his dominance status, the young buck has little choice but to interact with other males and achieve fraternal group membership. He must then compete with other males and rise in rank over his peers to eventually become a dominant herd sire.

In spring, social groups of whitetail bucks may be highly variable in size, depending upon male longevity, herd sex and age ratios, environmental conditions, and other factors. Where hunters intensively harvest antlered bucks, few if any bucks may survive to maturity, and fraternal groups may then be uncommon or even nonexistent.

Habitat characteristics may also influence fraternal

By the time they become reproductively mature, male deer are outcast by their mothers and their matriarchal clans. Young bucks then seek association with other males and eventually become members of a mixed age fraternal group.

group size, with larger groups or aggregations of fraternal groups forming only in open habitat. For instance, whitetail biologist Bennett Brown found fraternal groups to vary in size from two to as many as 17 individuals on the expansive grasslands of the Rob and Bessie Welder Wildlife Refuge in south Texas. He observed that the very large groups were quite unstable, however, and suggested that they may have been composed of combinations of several fraternal groups.

My own investigations conducted in northern Michigan indicate that fraternal groups tend to be small in heavily forested cover, even in lightly hunted areas. David Hirth made similar observations when comparing the behavior of deer in southern Michigan to that of deer on the open Texas grasslands. Although Hirth observed some large groups in open habitat, he noted that buck groups in dense cover normally comprised only two or three individuals.

Hirth proposed that variations seen in buck group size are related to cover density and predator avoidance: "The predator avoidance hypothesis holds that an animal as relatively large as most ungulates is more likely to avoid detection by a predator in dense cover when it is alone or in small groups. In dense cover, a single animal can be effectively concealed, whereas this concealing effect [in dense cover] is lost with a larger group

or herd. In open habitat, the reverse is true. Most ungulates are too large to be able to feed in the open and be concealed from potential predators at the same time. For that reason, species that normally utilize open grassland habitat typically occur in larger groups or herds. In a large group, the collective senses of many animals can be used to detect approaching predators, and the probability that a given animal will be selected by a predator is reduced by a factor roughly equal to the number of animals in the group."

During spring, several fraternal groups may share a relatively large range of several hundred acres, especially if spring flora and other nutritious herbaceous growth is concentrated in certain habitats. Even in heavily forested cover, five to 10 bucks then might occasionally intermingle. Close visual observations or monitoring by means of radio-telemetry will generally reveal, however, that only two or three socially bonded individuals — true fraternal companions — consistently travel and feed together. These socially bonded individuals also retreat to rest in their small, preferred areas within the larger range shared by several such groups.

During this relatively peaceful period, a dominant buck may sometimes travel freely over a large range occupied by several fraternal groups. Often referred to as a "dominant floater," this wandering male periodically associates with each buck in the area. In spring and early summer, bucks avoid antagonistic interactions that might damage their tender, velvet antlers. At this time of year, too, blood levels of testosterone, the male hormone that precipitates aggression, are at a low ebb. Consequently, to maintain dominance over familiar subordinate bucks and to minimize aggressive antler contact, the superior male need merely perform subtle threat displays, such as the ear-drop and hard-look combination.

Whitetail bucks effectively employ visual signals when in close contact with other deer. But, in dense cover, their glandular secretions and scent deposits, referred to as chemical signals, probably play an even more important, longer lasting, communicative role. According to researchers Karl Miller and Larry Marchinton, "Sources of communicative odors in deer include specialized skin glands, the urine, vaginal secretions, and possibly saliva. Researchers have identified at least eight areas of a deer's body that have specialized development of glandular tissues likely to be involved in scent communication."

Although investigated most thoroughly during the whitetail's breeding season, scent marking plays a prominent communicative role in the whitetail's social life throughout the year.

In autumn, mature bucks establish signposts, more popularly referred to as buck "rubs," made when they rub particular trees with their antlers (and forehead); and "scrapes," produced when they paw spots on the ground and urinate on them, and scent-mark overhead tree branches. These signs, which involve both visual and chemical stimuli, serve to communicate the maker's dominance, individual identity, and other information of social significance. These signposts are primarily made prior to and during the breeding season, but sometimes certain components are made during other seasons as well. I've observed highly aggressive dominant bucks rub trees and shrubs with their forehead during spring, after casting (dropping) their antlers. Although they left no visible rub marks, as normally occurs when they debark trees with their hardened antlers, the bucks presumably left secretions from their forehead glands on the rubbed stems as chemical evidence of their high social status. Nonetheless, I'm unaware of any scientific evidence documenting the significance of such forehead scent-marking of stems, small trees, or shrubs during the spring season.

A full scrape is a highly complex whitetail signpost, and making one integrates various behaviors and probably serves multiple purposes. Most full scrapes are made by dominant bucks and include the following major components: (1) overhead limb mutilation

Whitetail bucks maintain communication with other deer by scent marking trees, branches, and soil with a variety of chemical secretions.

and scent-marking; (2) ground pawing; and (3) urination, sometimes combined with tarsal gland rubbing (referred to as rub-urination). Because the scrape is such a complex signpost, and because bucks make certain components of the scrape throughout the year, researchers speculate that many different messages are involved and that the messages probably change seasonally. The precise signals conveyed by the chemical secretions, or "pheromones," deposited at the scrape, however, remain a subject of debate.

Adult bucks exhibit gentle limb-marking, ground pawing, and rub-urination independently or in combination year-round. However, the acts of pawing and mutilating overhead limbs occur most frequently during the breeding season when bucks carry hardened antlers. The consensus among researchers is that scent-marking of overhead limbs communicates a buck's identity. (Although it has not been specifically documented, glandular secretions from the forehead, preorbital area, and nose, in combination with saliva, are probably used in limb-marking. Some members of the deer family even use their velvet antlers to transfer body secretions to signpost limbs.)

Bucks of all social ranks reportedly mark branches, even during the non-reproductive period, and investigate those marked by other bucks. Also, some but not all of the overhead limbs marked during the spring and summer become scrapes during autumn.

The amount of scent-marking and scraping demonstrated by whitetail bucks in spring may vary regionally. My observations indicate that, at least on northern range where deer migrate seasonally, bucks intensively scent-mark their favored summer habitat, sometimes even with the full scrape sequence, as soon as they return in spring. I speculate that such marking helps bucks reclaim familiar habitat that has been devoid of deer for several months.

In spring, when south-facing slopes start to lose their snow cover, whitetail bucks return to summer habitat and begin scent marking their favorite haunts.

Scrape making is considered an important part of the whitetail's autumn rutting behavior. The manufacture of a full scrape is dependent upon physiological changes acting upon the buck in autumn, especially increased testosterone production, as are other physical and behavioral changes associated with breeding. Logically, then, one might ask the question: Why should bucks scrape at all during the spring period when testosterone levels are supposedly at their lowest level?

There may be a firm physiological basis to explain the scraping behavior demonstrated by mature whitetail bucks in spring. According to George Bubenik, a prominent researcher from the University of Guelph, in Ontario, there is evidence showing that whitetail bucks exhibit a brief surge in testosterone production with increasing photoperiod during spring. Conceivably, such hormonal stimulation (probably in April and May) could account for a brief but substantial increase in male-male aggression and associated scent-marking behavior by dominant individuals.

There is a natural tendency for the adult sexes to avoid one another while does are raising fawns and bucks are growing antlers. One reason for this avoidance may be that the sexes then have different food and cover needs; another is that does become secretive and solitary while raising fawns.

Also, because adult bucks heavily scent-mark their traditional summering grounds, especially during the spring period, pregnant does might be intimidated by such odors and less likely to settle on buck-occupied range. If so, scent marking by bucks during spring could assist in segregating the sexes, help maintain social harmony, reduce resource competition, and enhance fawn-rearing success.

Whatever the reasons, shortly before giving birth, most adult does retreat to their ancestral summering grounds to raise their fawns. And for several months, commencing with the birth of fawns, antler-growing bucks avoid contact with adult does and settle down on their favored summering grounds.

YEARLING BEHAVIOR

Although whitetails are usually weaned by 12 weeks of age, they tend to spend their first year in close association with their mothers. Having adult leadership is especially important for those young deer that live in northern regions and migrate long distances between summer and winter ranges. Since lengthy migratory routes are learned, young-of-the-year whitetails must have guidance to find favorable wintering habitat. Before their own migratory traditions are fully ingrained, they must also be led back to their distant summer ranges in spring. Because sexually immature whitetails live in a matriarchal society, however, any migration-wise female relative may provide the necessary guidance should the mother die during autumn or winter.

When they return to their summer range, mother and offspring associate closely until shortly before the mother's new fawns are born. A few days before giving birth, the doe isolates herself by driving away all other deer, including her year-old (yearling) fawns.

Although interactions leading up to separation of the mother from her yearling offspring have been poorly documented, rather violent, pugnacious actions by the mother are probably necessary to sever the close social bonds a yearling has established with its mother. In anthropomorphic terms, maternally dependent offspring probably experience a certain amount of psychological trauma when their normally care-giving dam suddenly turns on them with aggressive fury and vengeance she has shown in the past when confronted by strange foe. Needless to say, from that point on, the yearling's social life changes considerably, but the duration of that change depends primarily upon its mother's subsequent fawn-rearing success.

Should the doe's newborn fawns die, for whatever reason, her aggressive temperament subsides shortly thereafter. Within a few days after the death of her newborn, the mother resumes a sociable lifestyle and tolerates the companionship of her yearling offspring, as well as that of older, nonproductive daughters. In that event, the doe, accompanied by her yearlings and possibly an older doe or two, travels a larger range and will likely center her activity in a different part of her home range.

Aside from bucks in rut and does raising young fawns, whitetails seem to prefer some companionship, and the yearling suddenly driven away by its mother is no exception. When does are successful in raising fawns, yearlings generally seek other associates for a period of at least four to six weeks before they can reunite with their mothers. During that interval of mother-yearling separation, the yearlings might associate with nonproductive older female relatives, buck groups, others their same age or, more rarely, live alone.

Especially in productive habitat on northern range, mixed groups of male and female yearlings are quite common during late spring and summer. Generally, these groups are composed of from two to five related individuals — siblings or cousins — that had associated with one another during the previous autumn and winter periods. (In regions where bucks are heavily exploited by hunting and few mature bucks exist, there is a tendency to refer to groups of yearling males as fraternal groups; technically, however, they are not.)

For unknown reasons, according to Hirth, groups comprised exclusively of yearlings rarely form in the savanna grasslands of Texas. Instead, in such open habitat, yearlings more commonly join doe groups, mixed groups of bucks, does, and fawns, or sometimes even buck groups during summer. It may be noteworthy, however, that mortality of newborn fawns was extremely high in Hirth's south Texas study area (often due to excessive depredation by coyotes), which could have meant that more of the fawnless does accepted companionship.

In heavily forested cover typical of northern Michigan, I found that most nonreproductive yearlings (male and female) occupy the free-travel corridors that normally exist between adjacent doe-fawning territories. Whatever the mechanisms involved, the yearlings seem to quickly recognize and soon avoid traveling into adjacent, protected fawning areas while on familiar ancestral range.

Male and female siblings generally remain together throughout summer, but males are more likely to take off on brief exploratory jaunts several miles into strange habitat. In fact, some male fawns may achieve puberty when seven or eight months old, exhibit advanced

physiological and behavioral development, and join buck groups when one year old.

In areas of high deer productivity and limited forest cover, springtime behavior of young deer may differ considerably from that observed in forested cover. One reason for this differential behavior is that half or more of the females in these populations may breed when six to seven months old, meaning that they too must find favorable fawn-rearing habitat, probably during early summer. According to Nixon, on the intensively farmed land of the Midwest, about half of the fawns may

In open grasslands, unlike in thick, forested habitats, whitetails form mixed groups of bucks, does, and yearlings.

disperse at 10 to 12 months of age to new range. "Unlike deer in northern forests," says Nixon, "where seasonal movements of fawns and home range selection are dictated by their mothers' movements, most farm belt females and fawn males undertake these dispersals and migrations without kin support and prior social experience and learning. Suitable habitats to support these inexperienced deer are scarce in spring because preferred sites (likely upland shrub and successional forests) are already occupied by older deer. Row crops are as yet too young to provide cover, and hay and wheat crops, which could shelter deer, are no longer abundant."

Even in heavily forested northern Minnesota, where deer densities are fairly low, Nelson and Mech found that some yearling females dispersed to new range during spring. In their studies, Nelson and Mech determined that 20 percent of the yearling does dispersed from 10 to 100 miles to new ranges about the time their mothers produced new fawns, or shortly thereafter. Reasons for such movement were undetermined but presumed to be "voluntary and independent of density," because deer densities were comparatively low and favorable cover plentiful.

Depending primarily upon their own degree of sexual maturity and their mother's fawn-rearing success, then, the spring behavior of yearling whitetails will vary a great deal from one region to another. In some situations they will exhibit an advanced rate of behavioral development, disperse to new ranges, and assume lives more like those of older deer. At other times, however, they will remain on ancestral range in close contact with female relatives and will live more subdued, immature lifestyles.

Where forest cover is limited, yearling does must disperse to find unoccupied fawn-rearing habitat. Some young does may disperse as much as 100 miles from ancestral range in doing so.

The understory of a forest comes alive in spring. Ferns, grasses and forbs offer deer a break from their tedious diet of winter. Even mushrooms and other nontraditional deer foods are welcome sights to whitetails in spring.

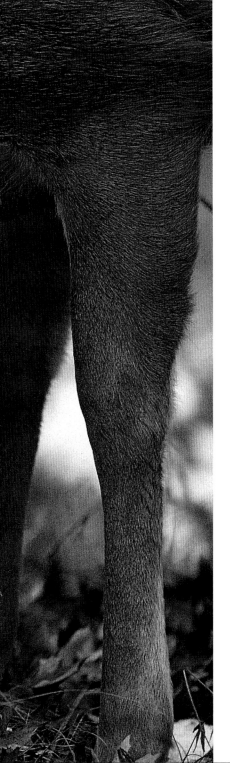

NUTRITION AND FEEDING

Whitetails are adapted to eating vegetation. They are ruminants — cud chewers — and possess a compound, four-chambered stomach. Their digestive system allows for fast and selective food gathering, a large capacity for food storage, and leisurely cudding and chewing.

Microfauna and microflora that live in their rumen, the first and largest chamber of the compound stomach, break down fibrous plants the deer ingest. The fermentation process, the enzymatic action in the rumen that breaks down cellulose and complex carbohydrates into digestible components, makes ruminants much different than simple-stomached animals.

Fat stored during autumn provides whitetails reserve energy to be used during winter when weather is harsh and good food is limited. Whitetails also go into a depressed physiological state during winter, when their metabolism

As the days lengthen in spring, whitetails' metabolism increases significantly. Finding and eating nutritious food will now become the animals' predominant activity.

decreases and they become very inactive in order to conserve energy.

Beginning about mid-March, however, coincident with the lengthening of daylight hours, whitetails become more active. Their metabolism rises as well, and their food requirements increase.

Indeed, whitetail spring is a nutritionally demanding time of year for all deer, and the consequences of inadequate spring nutrition are many, ranging from subtle physical impairments to death.

SELECTIVE FEEDERS

Whitetails are highly selective feeders when nutritious foods are available. They must be selective in their foraging because they are smaller than most other ruminants. Unlike cattle or large grazing ruminants, deer have comparatively less rumen storage capacity and less ability to digest highly fibrous or lignified materials. Normally, deer will nuzzle or hold plant parts in their mouth, swallowing those that are succulent and easily digestible, but rejecting others that are dry and high in fiber.

The whitetail's pointed snout and dentition are adapted for meticulously selecting plants and plant parts. According to Montana research biologist Larry Dusek, "A narrow mouth, the small, narrow incisors, and a hard, bony pad in place of upper incisors allow the deer to select and snip off the tender tips of woody plants and the buds and leaves of herbaceous forage. With its dexterous lips and tongue, the deer selects its food, then uses its lower incisors and bony pad like a pair of scissors to sever the morsel from the plant. Deer are thus able to select not merely what plants they eat but even which specific parts of those plants."

It's important to note that diet selection by deer cannot be based on any single factor. Digestibility is sometimes important in determining what plants deer

Nutritious food in large quantities is essential to whitetails in spring. Not only must they replace body reserves utilized over winter, new energy demands, such as molting and replacing the winter coat and growing antlers, place great caloric requirements on deer.

will or won't eat, but digestibility cannot explain plant preferences in all cases.

The nutritional requirements of individual deer differ depending upon their sex, age, reproductive condition, and other factors, and change rather dramatically with the seasons. Plant species also vary a great deal in their total nutrient make-up, and plants low in certain nutrients are sometimes high in others.

There are many complex nutritional relationships that make diet diversity important for whitetails. In spring, for example, the calcium requirements of deer are high. And although certain plants may be poorly digested and pass through the deer's digestive system rapidly, they may be selected by deer for their high calcium content. Also, eating certain plants tends to aid in the digestion of others. Researchers have learned that although some plants may be high in protein or digestible energy, they are too low in nitrogen, phosphorus, magnesium, or sulfur for adequate rumen function. But such nutrient-deficient plants may be utilized if they are eaten in combination with other plants high in the deficient elements.

There is also evidence that deer can detect and avoid eating compounds that inhibit the action of rumen microorganisms. At low concentrations, these so-called "secondary compounds" seem to have little or no impact upon rumen function, making whitetails' habit of eating small amounts of a variety of plants a natural safeguard against consuming too much of any toxic substance.

The whitetail's diverse nutritional requirements largely explain why deer forage the way they do. That's why they walk along slowly, eating "some of this" combined with "a little of that," thereby selecting the proper mix of nutrients to meet their immediate dietary needs.

Fortunately, the whitetail's digestive tract can change with its diet. The size of the rumen, the character of the rumen lining, saliva production, microbe composition and abundance, and other features of a whitetail's digestive system change with the seasons, depending upon the nutritive value of the foods consumed. This is especially important during the spring season when rising temperatures stimulate the growth of new, herbaceous forage, because whitetails' normally poor, highly fibrous, late winter and early spring diet soon changes to one that is highly nutritious and easily digested.

SPRING FOOD

White-tailed deer will consume a wide variety of foods, including grasses, sedges, fruits, nuts, forbs and mushrooms, in addition to leaves and twigs of trees and shrubs. Depending upon food availability, they will occasionally even eat insects, birds, and fish.

There are probably hundreds of items that whitetails eat during spring, foods that vary regionally according to climate and soil types. Rich soils will provide natural forage and agricultural crops high in protein, carbohydrates, sugars, fats, minerals, and essential vitamins, while infertile soils will provide forage of lower nutritive value. To my knowledge, however, no one has ever compiled a complete list of deer foods and likely never will. In fact, it would probably be easier to list natural items deer do not eat.

Their diet in spring is probably more diversified, in terms of quantity and quality, than it is during any other time of the year; it can change rather sharply within a few days, as governed by soil type, rate of snow melt, temperature, amount of moisture, and other factors. On northern range, the whitetails' diet will likely change from being nutritionally poor to excellent within a few weeks, and sometimes within a matter of a few days, when temperatures rise and snow melts in spring.

Even individual plant species and plant parts change greatly in their nutritive value with maturity. Certain forbs, grasses, and sedges may be succulent and highly digestible when they first appear, but become hardened and fibrous at maturity. Even certain nutritious agricultural crops such as winter wheat and alfalfa become less digestible as they mature. On the other hand, new leaves of trees and shrubs are much more nourishing than the buds and woody twigs deer subsist upon during winter.

In the Upper Great Lakes region, as soon as snow melts on south-facing slopes and around the bases of trees in the uplands, deer supplement their woody browse diets with leaves of small plants that remain green beneath the snow. According to data compiled by U.S. Forest Service research biologist Lynn Rogers and his coworkers, bunchberry, wintergreen, strawberry, and barren strawberry are preferred early spring deer foods. As spring progresses, new green grass, emerging forbs, and new

Throughout winter, even on northern range, certain low-growing plants remain green beneath the snow. Come snow melt, wintergreen and strawberry are some of the first foods available to hungry whitetails.

Besides wild strawberry (above), the early spring diet of whitetails may include a diversity of small plants, twigs, shoots, and dried leaves.

leaves of trees and shrubs become more important, and then represent about 90 percent of the whitetail's diet.

Other highly preferred spring foods of whitetails in the Great Lakes states and in the Northeast include goldenrod, clover, adder's tongue, buttercup, dandelion, Dutchman's breeches, swamp fern, violets, false Solomon's seal, marsh marigold, and common yarrow. Even certain aquatic plants, such as bur reeds, certain algae, ribbonleaf pondweed, water horsetail, arrowhead, pond lilies, and marsh cinquefoil are nutritionally important to whitetails in some areas. Aside from being easily digested and high in protein, aquatic plants also tend to be high in sodium and other important minerals and vitamins.

While following tame whitetails in Maine, Hewlette Crawford, working for the U. S. Forest Service, documented sharp changes in the spring diet of whitetails around the time of snowmelt. "Herbaceous plants were not important as a source of deer food during winter," noted Crawford. "As the snow left the ground in early spring, the animals began to eat ferns, sedges, green leaves of lambkill kalmia, wintergreen, and trailing arbutus, dried leaves of swamp dewberry, American beech twigs, and other species in small amounts, while continuing to eat red maple twigs and dried leaves and northern white cedar green shoots."

According to Crawford, "During late spring, forbs accounted for nearly three-fourths of the [whitetails'] diet. Blue beadily and Canada beadruby accounted for more than 50 percent, by weight, of all plants eaten during late spring. Sedges, ferns, red maple twigs, and red raspberry shoots also were important components."

The importance of diversity in the whitetails' diet is not restricted to northern regions. In the Missouri Ozarks, for example, Larry Vangilder and other researchers from the University of Missouri found that the chemical and structural composition of spring deer foods were highly variable and that different forage types satisfied different nutritional needs. The researchers reported that "forbs and grasses had high digestibility and contained high levels of protein, phosphorus, and potassium. Leaves of woody species, although poorly digested, provided significant amounts of rapidly fermented cell solubles, had a high calcium content, and probably were rapidly passed through the digestive system. Fruits of woody species were high in energy."

From a practical standpoint, the Missouri research emphasized that deer have evolved the ability to select a mix of forages that balance nutritional demands. In the investigators' words: "Forages cannot be ranked low in quality because they do not meet all the nutritional demands of white-tailed deer ... The results reaffirm the

To obtain all the essential amino acids required for growth and maintenance, whitetails must eat a wide variety of foods in spring, from wildflower leaves and blossoms (above) to the succulent new leaves of red maple (below).

traditional wildlife management concept of retarding plant succession to increase plant species diversity. Habitat for white-tailed deer in nonagricultural areas such as the Missouri Ozarks should be managed to stimulate the production of a great diversity of forbs, fruits, and leaves of woody species if the carrying capacity of the range is to be increased. Management practices that favor a single species or one forage type (such as agricultural food plots) should be avoided."

Harry Jacobson, professor of wildlife management and a noted whitetail researcher from Mississippi State University, reports that important spring foods of whitetails in the Southwest include prickly pear, lechuguilla, acacia, osage orange, grapes, sumac, oak, ash, and persimmon. In the Southeast, Jacobson reports, "Spring is a time of plenty, when deer consume succulent new growth of honeysuckle and trumpet creeper vines and herbaceous plants such as aster, mint, ragweed, nettle,

sedge, and a variety of aquatic plants."

Normally, fish are an infrequent, novel food item for whitetails. However, University of Michigan researchers David Case and Dale McCullough reported that deer on North Manitou Island in Lake Michigan learned to exploit and purposely sought out alewives, a sardine-sized fish that died and washed ashore in great numbers during spring and early summer. During peak periods of alewife die-off, the researchers estimated that from one-third to one-half of the total diet of deer on the island consisted of the small fish.

Case and McCullough concluded that the alewives were easily digested and highly nutritious for deer, being higher in crude protein, crude fat, and gross energy than natural deer forages available during the same period. While most natural forage the scientists examined on the island in late May and early June contained from three to five percent crude protein, the alewives provided over 22 percent.

The whitetails' spring diet varies by region. In the southwest, preferred foods include prickly pear cactus, acacia, osage orange, trumpet vine, honeysuckle, and persimmon (above).

These observations of deer eating fish are not meant to imply that such behavior is common, but it demonstrates the whitetails' adaptable nature and innate ability to take advantage of abundant nutritious food sources, as unusual as they may be.

Another poorly understood aspect of whitetails' nutritional requirements is their apparent salt hunger during the spring period. Whitetails are so readily attracted to salt during spring and early summer that researchers commonly use salt as bait in live traps to capture deer for special studies. Deer also make heavy use of natural min-

Following a prolonged, severe winter, green-up may come too late for malnourished deer. Despite the surfeit of new foods in spring, such winter-stressed animals may never recover from the ravages of winter.

eral licks at this time of year. Since high intake of sodium occurs in spring when deer increase their food consumption, some investigators speculate that high intake of potassium and water leads to excessive loss of sodium in the urine, hence the seasonal craving for salt.

Sodium is essential in many body functions, and sodium deficiency can lead to reproductive problems in some mammals. However, I know of no such evidence in whitetails.

MALNUTRITION

Although spring is usually considered a season of plenty for whitetails, there are exceptions. Not all whitetails are well nourished in spring, and some suffer severe consequences due to an inadequate diet.

On northern range, whitetails may face serious nutritional shortages in spring due to continued cold weather, prolonged snow cover, and delayed green-up. Massive starvation losses of deer may occur during those spring periods when heavy snow cover persists, confining deer to browsed-out deer yards into late April. Even when snowmelt does come, many weakened young deer, depleted of their energy reserves and suffering rumen damage, may migrate back to their summer ranges before dying.

Generally, however, the inadequacy of the spring

range may be easily overlooked, especially where persistently high deer densities have caused severe overbrowsing (and overgrazing) of the herbaceous forage. Because deer are highly selective feeders, continued heavy foraging may greatly reduce or even eliminate the most nutritious plants. Conversely, other plants may increase because they are less palatable, resistant to grazing, or both. In time, the land's nutritional base and capacity to naturally sustain healthy deer steadily declines with continued overuse.

Some areas have inherently infertile soils and produce forage that fails to meet the whitetails' high nutritional requirements during the spring period. The poorly drained and acidic soils of the flatwood habitats of northwestern Florida, for example, produce deer foods that average less than eight percent protein, which is below the level required for young whitetails for proper growth.

Whatever the reasons may be, poor nutrition during the spring period will impact the health and well-being of all deer. An inadequate spring diet will contribute to poor growth among young deer, retard antler growth among bucks, and provide poor fetal development, which ultimately leads to high newborn fawn mortality.

Marsh marigolds are but a small portion of the verdant growth available to deer in spring. Where soils are fertile and support many species of protein-rich plants, deer will thrive.

ANTLER GROWTH

Contrary to speculation by 18th century French scientist Comte De Buffon, deer antlers are not made of wood, even though they are normally branched and shed their outer covering. Antlers are true solid bone (they have no marrow cavity), and are only grown by members of the deer family, Cervidae. Antlers are uniquely mammalian; they are the only appendages that annually replace themselves, and their phenomenal growth rate even surpasses that of dreaded cancer.

Among white-tailed deer only the males normally grow antlers, a secondary sex characteristic that evolved hand-in-hand with other aspects of buck breeding behavior. (In reindeer and caribou, both sexes normally grow antlers.) Occasionally, however — probably about one among every few thousand individuals — female whitetails also grow antlers, generally due to a hormone imbalance.

The cycle of antler growth, hardening, casting (dropping

Where available, aquatic plants such as burr reeds, pondweeds, horsetail, arrowhead, and pond lilies are preferred whitetail foods. These plants contain large amounts of important minerals and vitamins necessary for antler growth.

A buck's antlers are magnificent ornaments, but they also advertise his strength to adversaries and his desirability as a mate to does.

off), and regrowth is controlled by hormones. This cycle involves a complex interplay between the tiny pineal gland, the hypothalamus of the brain, the pituitary gland, and the testes, and is a response to seasonal changes in the amount of daylight. The cycle follows the seasonal, rhythmic rise and fall in blood levels of the male hormone testosterone, which is produced principally by the testes.

"To the deer hunter, antlers are prized trophies," says Richard Goss, one of the world's foremost authorities on antler regeneration. Antlers are also referred to as "bones of contention," because of the amount of debate and controversy surrounding their growth and development.

"To the animal lover," says Goss, "they are magnificent ornaments adorning one of the world's most graceful animals. To the zoologist, they are fascinating curiosities that seem to defy the laws of nature. To the deer themselves, they are status symbols in the competition for male supremacy."

To say that antlers are unique structures grown by remarkable creatures is indeed an understatement. In Goss' words: "Antlers are an extravagance of nature rivaled only by such other biological luxuries as flowers, butterfly wings, and peacock tails. The antlers of deer are so improbable that if they had not evolved in the first place, they would never have been conceived even in the wildest fantasies of the most imaginative biologists."

THE PEDICLE

Antlers are actually two structures in one: the antler itself and the pedicle, or stump, on the ends of which the antler develops. Antlers drop off and are replaced annually; pedicles are permanently attached to the buck's head.

Before a deer can grow antlers, it must first grow pedicles. (If the buck fawn is castrated prior to reaching puberty he will not develop pedicles and will not grow antlers.) In young bucks, these pedicles may be as much as an inch long, but they shorten as the deer matures. According to Goss, when bucks are mature, the pedicles are "...remodeled into the expanding skull. In adults the antlers appear attached directly to the skull. Nevertheless, it is in the pedicle, or in the surrounding parts of the skull or scalp, that the tissues from which antlers are regenerated each year are located."

The cellular makeup of the pedicle differs from that of the surrounding cranium in that it is composed of spongy bone instead of compact bony plates. That pedicle formation is a prerequisite to producing antlers has been proven experimentally: Antlers have been induced to grow on leg bones or other parts of the deer's body by surgically transplanting pedicle tissue to new sites. Occasionally, too, auxiliary antlers, protruding from other parts of the fore-

head or upper orbit of a buck's eye, will occur naturally when its pedicles are severely damaged, possibly when fighting, resulting in the proliferation of pedicle cells to other areas of the forehead.

In very young fawns, prior to pedicle formation, a pair of cowlicks appears, and small bony lumps can be felt beneath the skin where the future antlers will grow. Although they seldom grow antlers, even young female whitetails possess these lumps in their forehead bones, because they too are endowed with the potential to grow antlers.

Although the antler cycle itself is strictly programmed

As a young buck continues to mature, his pedicles enlarge, and the tips become covered with shiny skin and sparse hairs. Pedicle development is initiated with increased testosterone production.

Some early-maturing buck fawns will grow tiny "button antlers" by their first autumn. These will be cast in winter, much like adult bucks cast their antlers. Generally, though, most bucks start growing their first real set of antlers when about 11 months old.

by seasons and light cycles, development of the pedicle is not. Pedicle formation is linked more to the young animal's rate of maturity and to the production of testosterone, which stimulates additional bone deposition at the pedicle site.

The age at which the pedicle is first distinguishable depends upon the deer species and its environment. In some species, such as elk and caribou, the bases of the pedicle appear in the fetus during the second half of gestation. In white-tailed deer, however, pedicles develop after birth and usually don't become pronounced "bumps" until the fawn is about four or five months old. This is the age at which a healthy young male's testes develop and start producing sufficient quantities of testosterone, prompting enlargement of the pedicles.

At first, the pedicles are covered with skin and hair, similar to the tissue covering the rest of the deer's scalp. As the pedicles enlarge, however, the tips more closely resemble the growing antlers of adult bucks. The skin then becomes shiny and only sparsely covered with hairs that grow at right angles to it. Associated with each hair follicle is a sebaceous gland from which an oily secretion (sebum) is produced. Goss suggests that this sebum, which may contain pheromones, is responsible for the shiny appearance of the velvet skin. Some researchers have also suggested that the sebum may serve as an insect repellent, but such theory has not been proven.

According to noted scientist George Bubenik, "One of the unsolved questions in antler development is the fact that testosterone seems to promote growth of the pedicle but retards growth of antlers." That is, an elevation in testosterone must be achieved before the young male can develop pedicles during autumn. However, in adult deer, antlers start growing in spring when testosterone production is low. In these mature deer, high levels of testosterone during early autumn cause antlers to cease growing and mineralize.

Clearly, pedicle development is under strict hormonal and nerve control. Young deer must be born on schedule and be properly nourished in order to achieve a certain threshold body weight and level of maturity before the testes can produce enough testosterone to initiate pedicle formation. Also, although poorly documented, even social stress, or "crowding," may lead to excessive production of cortisol or other hormones that can block the effects of testosterone and impair pedicle development. In the absence of testosterone, or the presence of the female hormone estrogen, no pedicles form, and antlers fail to develop later on.

Lack of pedicle development in a given year usually is not a permanent condition; elevated testosterone production in subsequent years can stimulate pedicle and antler development. Buck fawns that fail to grow pedicles prior to winter, then, must grow them the next spring, when they are nearly one year old, before antler growth can commence. Obviously, since growth and maturation of the antlers are controlled by daylight cycles, these retarded animals simply do not have sufficient time to grow pedicles as well as sizable antlers; consequently, they invariably grow very small antlers at yearling age.

INFANT ANTLERS

Most bucks start growing their first antlers in spring, when about 11 months old. However, some large, well-developed buck fawns grow prominent pedicles topped with small "button" (infant) antlers less than one-half inch long during autumn, when about six or seven months of age. The infant antlers — a sign of rapid maturation and achievement of puberty — are cast during winter before new antler growth starts.

The transformation of the pedicle tip to antler is poorly understood. "Because it is such a gradual process," explains Goss, "it is impossible to pinpoint the exact point when pedicle growth gives way to antler development. The (origin) of the first antlers is a phenomenon that is not conveniently classified. Although the histological events undoubtedly resemble those by which subsequent sets of antlers are regenerated each year, the process is not an example of regeneration because there has been nothing lost to be replaced . . . In this respect, the fawn's initial antler is a unique zoological structure."

In effect, fawns that grow infant antlers achieve certain threshold levels of testicular development and testosterone production indicative of puberty. They then grow their second set of antlers at yearling age. These early maturing fawns are undoubtedly physically superior in all respects as compared to fawns that fail to grow pedicles or do not grow infant antlers.

ANTLER REGENERATION

"The most fundamental attribute of living things is that they can repair themselves," says Goss. "However, true regeneration is the replacement of missing parts of the adult organism. The annual regrowth of antlers is a special case of this general phenomenon."

Before antler regeneration can start, antlers must

mature, die, and be cast. As soon as the old antlers drop off, normally during winter, the swollen ring of skin around the pedicle grows over the stump of the antler — a process referred to as "wound healing." It's important to note that scar tissue does not form when skin grows over the freshly exposed pedicle. Also, the skin that forms is different in appearance and texture from that which covers the periphery of the pedicle. Its shiny surface is more like that of antler velvet, into which it will ultimately develop.

Regrowth of antlers is regulated by photoperiod and is triggered by increasing day length in spring. Goss demonstrated the importance of changing light regimes in regulating antler growth in sika deer raised under controlled lighting. When light cycles were artificially shortened, the deer grew as many as three sets of antlers per year. When light cycles were lengthened, they only grew antlers every other year.

Technically speaking, however, Goss concluded that

Antlers grow at a rate unequaled by any structure in the animal world. White-tailed deer antlers may elongate by as much as a quarter of an inch per day.

The regrowth of antlers in spring is initiated by testosterone production. In turn, increased production of testosterone is triggered by the season's lengthening periods of sunlight.

Early in their development, antlers are quite soft and easily damaged.
Malformed antlers are usually the result of an injury to the tip of a
growing antler and its protective layer of velvet.

"antler replacement is triggered neither by shortening nor lengthening days, but by alteration of such change irrespective of the direction of the shift in photoperiod." His work suggests that an internal mechanism initiates the antler cycle but that seasonal changes in photoperiod regulate the cycle to 12 months.

Because day length is nearly constant at equatorial latitudes, deer living in tropical and subtropical habitats experience only slight seasonal changes in the amount of daylight. Therefore, they lack the photoperiod cues and thus the seasonal aspects of reproduction displayed by their northern cousins. In the tropics, does may breed and give birth, and bucks may carry hardened antlers, at any time of the year. Nonetheless, even in the tropics, individual male deer grow only one set of antlers each year, the timing of regrowth being determined largely by when the deer were born.

Goss suggests that "tropical deer have apparently lost the ability, or need, to monitor and react to seasonal changes in day length. Whatever may be the mechanism by which these animals measure the passage of each 12-month period, it is apparently independent of latitude and photoperiod." But, Goss confesses, "How they are aware that 12 months have elapsed in an aseasonal environment is a mystery."

In the Northern Hemisphere, bucks commence growing new antlers in spring. However, the exact timing of antler regrowth varies somewhat among individuals, depending upon their age and general health status. Healthy, mature bucks may show signs of bulging new antler growth in early April. By comparison, new antler growth among malnourished mature individuals and yearling bucks growing their first set of full-fledged antlers may be delayed from two to four weeks. (Coat molt generally follows the same pattern, with mature, healthy individuals being the first to don their red summer coats.)

The seasonal secretion of hormones responsible for antler growth is controlled by the pineal gland, a pea-sized organ located deep within the mid-portion of the brain. The major pineal hormone is considered to be melatonin, which suppresses the production of luteinizing hormone by the pituitary gland. High levels of luteinizing hormone suppress production of testosterone by the testes. Changes in light signals received through the eye send electrical messages to the pineal gland, thereby controlling melatonin production and, indirectly, testosterone production. As nights get longer, melatonin production increases. Hence, the pineal gland plays an important role in translating seasonal changes in day length into physiological and developmental events.

The male sex hormone testosterone is the primary

Unlike horns, which grow incrementally over the years, antlers grow, harden, and are cast and regenerated annually. Here a young deer inspects an antler cast by a buck whitetail during the previous winter.

hormone that controls antler growth, but numerous other hormones are also involved. The exact factors responsible for initiating antler growth in spring are still debated.

Early in their development, antlers are quite soft and easily damaged, as the newly formed inner substance consists of a cartilaginous material high in water content. Growth occurs at the tip, whereas calcification starts in the shaft of the antler. (The core remains moist and spongy until the antler is cast.) Since the velvet covering of growing antlers is richly endowed with sensory nerves, the velvet hairs seem to serve as touch-sensitive feelers that warn in advance of a pending collision, thereby helping to minimize velvet antler damage. Also, the arteries supplying blood to growing antlers have unusually thick walls. When severed, the thick muscular walls quickly constrict, thereby minimizing blood loss.

Antlers are the fastest-growing structures in the animal kingdom. (Moose antlers may elongate at the astounding rate of three-quarters of an inch per day; those of whitetails grow about one-quarter an inch per day.) Antlers begin growing rather slowly in spring, elongate rapidly during summer, and then slow in growth rate toward autumn. Although the live deer antler may remain velvet covered for about four to five months, most of the growth is accomplished during June and July. Complete elongation of the antler is normally completed within 100 days.

The high metabolic demand of antler growth requires a large blood supply to the growing tips. The blood flow is so great that the surface temperature of the antler is warm to the touch. In fact, velvet covered deer antlers are probably the only external mammalian structures in which the surface temperature equals that of the deep body. Hence, some scientists speculate that antlers may serve as "thermal radiators," so that bucks can dissipate surplus body heat during hot weather — a possible benefit but an unlikely hypothesis to explain the primary function of antlers.

THE ROLE OF NUTRITION

Despite the vast amount of research conducted on whitetails, the specific nutritional requirements for antler growth are only poorly understood. Logically, since antlers are regenerated bone, dietary factors that are important to bone growth must also be important to antler growth. Therefore, the amount of digestible energy, protein, calcium, phosphorus, and vitamins A and D in the buck's diet are assumed to be vital for proper antler growth.

It would seem rather simple to determine the chemical composition of deer antlers, then estimate the nutrients required to build such structures. Unfortunately, antler mineral composition varies according to the stage

Antler size and good nutrition are intricately linked. To grow large antlers, whitetail bucks need adequate food to satisfy the demands of body growth and maintenance as well as of growing antlers.

of growth — the composition of a mature (mineralized) antler is much different from that of an actively growing one. In red deer, for example, researchers found that 65 percent of the mineral found in mature antlers was deposited in the last 10 weeks of growth. Therefore, chemical analysis of antlers does not necessarily reveal the amount of dietary nutrients the animal must consume to build them.

Sharply contrasting seasonal patterns in food consumption by bucks also complicate matters when trying to determine nutrient requirements for antler growth. Bucks feed heavily during spring and summer, but they fast during the autumn breeding period. Mature rutting bucks may then lose 20 to 25 percent of peak body weight in a matter of four to six weeks. The energy-costly rut is followed by the harsh winter season when the quantity of high-quality food is limited and whitetails voluntarily restrict their food consumption. Hence, in some environments, adult bucks survive on very limited or poor-quality nutrition for five to six consecutive months.

The production of antlers is a tremendous drain on the buck's system. Some investigators even suggest that a buck's nutrient requirements for growing antlers are as great as those of a doe nursing fawns.

According to Goss, there are two ways that growing antlers could affect mineral balance in the buck's body:

"One would be for the deer to consume extra quantities of salts during the period when the antlers are growing, thereby depositing materials directly into the developing antlers. Alternatively, such minerals might be incorporated into the other bones of the body, later to be withdrawn and reutilized in antler construction. Investigators have confirmed that the latter mechanism is the method by which minerals are mobilized for antler growth."

Therefore, although deer apparently do not store excess minerals in the skeleton in anticipation of antler growth, they do accelerate turnover of such substances — especially calcium and phosphorus — during the antler-growing period. As a result, blood levels of the various minerals change only minimally on a seasonal basis. Even when fed supplemental diets high in calcium and phosphorus, bucks still undergo mineral depletion in their bones (especially their ribs, skull, and other bones that do not bear body weight) while growing antlers.

Assuming that buck fawns are adequately nourished during summer and autumn, and grow well, their level of nutrition during winter seems to have minimal effect upon their antler development at yearling age. However, body growth takes precedence over antler development; as discussed previously, any deficiency in energy, protein, calcium, phosphorus, or certain vitamins in the diet of young males can seriously retard their skeletal growth and delay pedicle development. Ultimately, bucks nutritionally deprived during early life are destined to grow undersized antlers at maturity.

Although certain study results are contradictory, investigations conducted in Michigan by Duane Ullrey revealed that the level of nutrition bucks experience during early spring, in the month before antler growth commences, greatly influences antler development. Ullrey varied the diets of captive animals to simulate early (March) versus late (April) green-up. The early green-up group had better body weights, antler weights, antler beam diameters, and main beam lengths. Ullrey's findings indicated that, in spring, early availability of energy-rich forage that is also high in protein improves antler development among young bucks.

Despite the many mysteries regarding antler growth among whitetails, one truism regarding these bones of contention prevails: "The head grows according to the pasture, good or otherwise." If male whitetails are well-nourished throughout life, most will grow respectable antlers at maturity. In contrast, underfed individuals are more likely to demonstrate poor body growth and delayed sexual maturity, and they tend to grow stunted antlers, even when mature, if subjected to continued poor nutrition.

Producing antlers places a tremendous drain on a male whitetail's metabolism. Some investigators suggest the nutrient requirements rival those placed on does nursing fawns.

Fawn-Rearing Behavior

In order to survive, fawns must be born at the proper time in spring when climatic conditions are favorable and food and cover are abundant. Also, where predators are abundant, births should be reasonably synchronized; many fawn births within a relatively short period of time results in what ecologists refer to as "prey saturation." With most of the fawns being born within a few weeks, predators are literally overwhelmed with potential prey. As a result, a higher percentage of the fawns survive the vulnerable hiding stage of early development.

It is important to note, therefore, that in addition to food and cover, space may also become a restrictive commodity in instances of high deer density or where tree and shrub cover is limited, as, for example, on intensively farmed land of the Midwest. And, as alluded to earlier in the discussion of female social organization, even the sequence of breeding among does within a matriarchal group probably evolved in such a way so as

In white-tailed deer, the quality and intensity of maternal care is governed by many factors; among others the doe's nutritional state and her status within her maternal clan will affect the well-being of her offspring.

to help set the stage for harmonious occupation of ancestral range for rearing fawns.

TERRITORIAL BEHAVIOR

Many if not most species of birds and mammals defend part of their home range against intrusion from other members of their species, at least during certain times of the year. This defended area is called a "territory." Territorial defense usually involves outright aggression by the property owner when its turf is trespassed upon by another of its kind.

My research conducted in Upper Michigan revealed that whitetail does with newborn fawns demonstrate a form of maternal defense, or territoriality, for a period of four to six weeks. Each doe with newborn then defends an exclusive area from which she drives away all other deer. Since no two does may simultaneously raise fawns in the same area, territorial behavior restricts the number of successful does in a given area of forested habitat. Surplus does must occupy marginal fawn-rearing habitat or move long distances to find favorable habitat.

By some definitions, a territory need not be a fixed piece of geography. It can "float." Under this definition, the animal defends only the area it happens to be in at the moment or during a certain season or day, or both. (Although I disagree, some investigators contend that whitetail mothers defend only the immediate area around the bedded fawn.) Other definitions have been equally vague, contributing to confusion of the concept as it applies to deer.

In trying to be more concise when defining the whitetail's territoriality, University of California researcher Floyd Weckerly suggested that the defended area should have resources that enhance reproductive success: "The defended area ... should be exclusive because enhancing reproductive success involves excluding [other deer]. Resources for deer are food, cover, water or fawning

During the fawning season, a doe with newborn will aggressively defend her traditional fawning territory, even against matriarchal clan members.

The spotted coats of these twin fawns, photographed shortly after parturition, effectively camouflage them in early spring.

sites." In his definition, Weckerly considers fawning sites as "discrete areas that contain resources (e.g., cover, habitat structure) that enhance survival of (newborns)."

Aggressive interactions among deer are expensive in terms of the amount of energy spent and the risk of injury involved. Being overly active and fighting also draws attention from alert predators. So, serious aggression among whitetails occurs primarily during specific times of the year and in special situations: when deer can afford it, and when being victorious is extremely important and well worth the effort and the risk.

Most violent encounters between whitetails occur in response to food or are related to the animal's stage of reproduction. Bucks may fight savagely during the autumn breeding period when they vie for dominance and breeding privileges. Deer of both sexes and all ages also fight over limited and concentrated food, especially in winter. During the fawning season, however, it is the doe with newborn on her traditional fawning grounds that becomes the aggressor, and all other deer the aggressed.

I might have had one of the most unique opportunities available to study the effects of increasing density on the behavior and population dynamics of whitetails. Using the herd inside the square-mile Cusino enclosure, I initiated a study in 1972 to evaluate the pros and cons of supplementally feeding deer to achieve populations higher than the habitat could naturally support. While allowing the herd to increase from 23 to 159 deer over a five-year period, I also studied the species' social organization and examined the consequences of social stress upon deer, independent of nutrition.

What made the enclosure studies so unique was that I could live-trap the entire herd each winter. Each animal was then weighed, measured, blood sampled to assess its physical condition and blood hormone levels, ear tagged, and marked with a numbered ear pennant for individual field recognition. But by far the most valuable data were gathered by X-raying does in March. Fetuses, then 80 to 140 days old, were readily detectable on radiograms. In addition to providing an exact count of the number of fawns the does carried, I also devised methods to age the fetus images with surprising accuracy.

Therefore, the X-ray technique permitted me to calculate probable breeding and birth dates, accurately determine potential fawn production, and when coupled with field observations, assess fawn-rearing success of individual does under tightly controlled nutritional and social conditions — something not possible in other studies of free-ranging deer.

Although the resultant herd size — about one deer per four acres — was 10 times the area's normal carrying capacity, I saw no behavioral or clinical signs of an impending population crash. Crowding did not result in dramatic density-dependent changes in deer physiology, as some investigators had proposed for other members of the deer family.

Once this test herd surpassed 100 deer per square mile, however, I recorded certain subtle changes in reproductive performance, such as delayed breeding and slightly lower fawning rates among young does. But the outstanding change was the steady rise in newborn fawn mortality among young does as deer density increased. At the herd's highest density — despite unlimited high-quality feed — prime-age does lost only six percent of their newborns, three-year-old does lost 24 percent of their newborns, and first-time mothers (two-year-olds) lost 63 percent of their newborns.

Indirect evidence from this study suggested that most fawns died shortly after birth and that losses were related to territorial behavior of does associated with fawn rearing. That is, because does with newborn fawns defend a territory of about 10 to 20 acres for about a month, crowding at peak deer density likely limited fawn-rearing space and disrupted maternal behavior. I concluded that heavy fawn mortality resulted from imprinting failure (mother to young or vice-versa) or outright abandonment of otherwise healthy offspring by socially stressed, inexperienced young mothers.

It's also interesting to note that the dominance rank of a young doe's relatives played a key role in determining fawn-rearing success when fawning space was limited in the enclosure. That is, during the final year of study, two-year-old does from the most dominant family group were able to raise five of seven fawns they carried, whereas similar-age does in more subordinate families raised only one of nine fawns they carried.

Those findings carry a number of intriguing

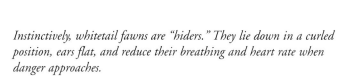

Instinctively, whitetail fawns are "hiders." They lie down in a curled position, ears flat, and reduce their breathing and heart rate when danger approaches.

implications. For example, observations indicate that dominant does are more successful in expanding their ancestral range. As a result, their family controls larger and superior ancestral fawning range. Regardless of their age, does associated with dominant families are less subject to social stress and are more likely to find suitable fawning sites, even when herd density is high.

Learning might also come into play. Conceivably, dominant does tend to produce female offspring that learn to be more aggressive, and therefore are better able to compete for limited fawning space.

Territorial behavior associated with fawning therefore constitutes an effective population self-regulation mechanism where nutritional shortage is not a potent factor in deer welfare. The number of fawn-rearing does in any given area is limited by space. Surplus does must therefore retreat to those habitats not particularly favorable for raising fawns, where more of their young will succumb to abandonment, accidents, or predation.

Hirth reported that deer living in the savanna grasslands of Texas behaved differently than those living in forested habitat of southern Michigan. In the open grasslands, does usually left their newborn fawns in hiding while they themselves grazed with other deer. The differing maternal care strategies, which apparently evolved in response to sharply contrasting environmental circumstances, allow whitetails in forested and nonforested habitats to cope most effectively with the constant threat that predation poses to the survival of their vulnerable offspring.

MATERNAL AGGRESSION

In some species, maternal aggression serves primarily to isolate the newborn and protect them from injury by others of the same species. In whitetails, isolating the young fawn assures that it will imprint on the mother, and not on strange deer. The mother normally imprints upon her fawn(s) within a few hours. However, the young may require several days before they become fully imprinted upon their mother. In addition, social isolation serves to reduce deer activity and associated odors in the vicinity of vulnerable fawns, thereby minimizing fawn detection by predators.

Unlike at other times of the year, the doe's aggressive behavior during the fawning season is probably less visible, primarily because the attentive mother is so secretive. She is most likely to make her presence known only when others of her species intrude into her cherished fawning grounds, or when a predator threatens the well-being of her young. Sometimes, however, she may be less secretive and browse casually in full view, when a

human observer can be reasonably assured that her fawns are not close by.

The doe's aggressive behavior associated with territorial defense differs from that she displays during other times of the year. Normally, conflicts involving does serve primarily to decide dominance-submissive relationships; these contests end abruptly once one of the deer involved exhibits submissive behavior. In contrast, territorial defense generally involves chasing, as the irate doe strives to evict the intruder from her fawn-rearing territory. In doing so, she initially employs a "head-high threat," with her chin pulled in and neck erect, combined with laying the ears back and staring at the intruder. When within 20 to 30 feet of one another, the doe likely rushes at her adversary, running behind it and kicking out with her front feet, sometimes pursuing for several hundred feet or until she is satisfied that the other deer is outside of her territory.

Related does know one another intimately and live within a firmly established dominance hierarchy on range they've probably occupied for a number of years. Each mature doe knows its place, generally uses the same fawn-rearing area year after year, and can probably identify territorial boundaries of relatives, based upon odors of their urine, feces, or even certain glandular secretions. Therefore, scent-marking may suffice to discourage other deer from trespassing upon a hostile doe's fawning grounds, simultaneously eliminating the need for conflict.

It's also important to note that a doe's territorial boundaries, and probably those of the entire clan, and the dominance relationships that formed the boundaries may have become established several years in the past. Where certain regions are occupied by whole families of related females, the ancestral range might pass on to descendants by tradition, with boundary disputes occurring only once in several generations. As members of a clan die, voids occur that are more likely filled by ancestral stock rather than dispersers from outside the area.

Aggression among related does for fawning space is probably minimal when deer densities are low. Moreover, when deer populations are below the carrying capacity of the environment, territorial defense may be muted or temporarily suspended altogether.

If many members of a clan die without producing enough daughters to carry on the occupation of traditional range, unrelated does from surrounding, crowded regions might move in to vie for fawning space. Territorial conflicts should be observed more frequently when does move into a new region or when deer densities are very high.

A day or two before giving birth, a pregnant doe may lick her flanks with uncommon frequency. Pacing about with a raised tail is another indication a doe is about to drop her fawn or fawns.

DOE DISPERSAL

Second-time mothers, generally those that are three years old, tend to disperse from their birthing area to establish new fawn-rearing territories. Likewise, when doe fawns breed and successfully rear fawns, they tend to disperse when two years old.

Depending on habitat availability and herd composition, dispersers likely shift their fawn-rearing areas a quarter mile or more from their birthing location. This serves to expand the ancestral range when conditions are favorable for population growth. However, dispersal is risky business because the dispersing doe may encounter considerable competition for space when seeking new fawning grounds. The disperser might settle in unsuitable fawning habitat or attempt to rear fawns within another doe's territory. This is especially true when deer densities are high. As a result, dispersing does normally experience much higher newborn fawn losses as compared to nondispersing individuals.

Rather unusual dispersal traits were reported by Charles Nixon and his co-workers for female whitetails living in intensively farmed areas of Illinois. Roughly half of the doe fawns and over 20 percent of the yearling does dispersed an average of 30 miles each spring.

This occurred in an area where deer typically enjoy excellent nutrition (about 75 percent of the doe fawns and all yearling does usually breed) but where forest cover and fawn-rearing habitat is very limited. Because hiding cover is limited, deer experience high mortality during hunting seasons, and many young does living in unhunted areas must disperse long distances in spring to find isolated pockets of forest cover devoid of deer to raise their fawns. Finding vacant fawning space usually is not a problem for the dispersers, and they tend to be very successful in raising fawns. In such cases, however, members of female clans cannot merely expand their ancestral range. Instead, young does must sever ties with relatives, seek new range, and find new associates.

At least one mature doe in Nixon's study dispersed to a new fawning range after her small woodlot fawning territory had been clear-cut. This single example suggests that certain land management practices may create problems for whitetail does, especially when their traditional fawning sites are severely altered or destroyed.

GIVING BIRTH

On northern range, most whitetail fawns are born in late May or early June, following a 200-day gestation. However, since doe fawns normally breed in December, most of their fawns are born in late June or early July. Peak fawning in southern states is a week to several weeks later, where it is also more protracted. In

Immediately after a fawn is born, the doe will spend from three to six hours at the birth site. One of her first maternal duties is licking the amniotic membranes and fluids from her offspring.

Mississippi, for example, peak fawning occurs in June and July, but some births may occur as early as April or as late as November.

The maternally experienced doe returns to the vicinity of her traditional fawning grounds several days, or even weeks, before giving birth. If healthy, she will show some signs of udder enlargement two weeks prior to giving birth. A few days before giving birth, she isolates herself by driving away all other deer, including her year-old offspring.

There is evidence that the doe has some control over when she gives birth. Hence, she has the opportunity to be fairly site-selective and choose where her fawns will be born. Observations indicate, however, that the doe may give birth anywhere in her chosen area, sometimes in grassy openings, but at other times in heavily wooded or dense brushy cover. Extremely wet sites seem to be avoided. Should a predator happen along, the doe can presumably hold off giving birth for a brief period until danger passes, but while in labor she is extremely vulnerable to predation.

In captivity, the first clear signs of a doe's imminent

Fawns are born with front feet and head first. The doe may give birth while standing or lying down. Immediately after the fawn is dropped, the mother will eat the afterbirth and lick birth fluids off the ground and from the fawn, removing any traces of scent that could attract predators.

parturition include pacing and tail elevation, which may appear from 24 to 48 hours before giving birth. Fawns are born, front feet and head first, while the doe is in a prostrate position, or they may be "dropped" while the doe is standing.

Normally, siblings are born about 15 to 20 minutes apart and at the same birth site. Although twins are the rule, triplets are relatively common among well-nourished deer, and litters of four and five fawns have been reported. Young does and malnourished individuals more commonly produce singletons, or possibly no fawns at

all. Contrary to the "old dry doe" myth, however, even healthy does 12 years of age and older regularly produce viable offspring. Although not a common occurrence, some does die during difficult births.

The mother spends from three to six hours following parturition at the birth site with her newborn — a precariously dangerous period for the young if predators are in the vicinity. She cleans them of amniotic fluids and membranes and carefully consumes all traces of the afterbirth (a trait not exhibited by all members of the deer family). She even eats the vegetation stained during

The doe above has already given birth to one of a pair of twin fawns. While she lies in labor, delivering her second offspring, the first fawn is already attempting to stand.

Siblings are normally born about 20 minutes apart. This doe has just delivered her second fawn and is consuming the afterbirth.

the birth process, often rendering the picked-over site quite recognizable as such, at least to the trained eye. The primary purpose of this careful cleansing serves to minimize odors that might otherwise attract predators. It may also be important in imprinting the mother to her young. However, some scientists speculate that the ingested amniotic membranes might supply the doe with certain important nutrients.

The fawn nurses almost immediately, probably for about four minutes, generally while the mother lies on her side. Colostrum milk, the high-protein secretion produced by the doe for a short time after giving birth, also provides the antibodies necessary to resist disease until the fawn's own immune system begins to function.

Isolation of the mother and newborn and the doe's grooming of the fawn shortly after birth are essential in establishing the mother-infant bond. Any disturbance during this critical period can lead to a breakdown in the imprinting process and can contribute to abandonment and death of the young. The risk is greatest when young, maternally inexperienced does are involved. Although the mother seems to imprint upon her young within a

Both fawns are cleaned and groomed by the doe immediately after birth. This type of maternal caregiving helps strengthen the critical doe-fawn bond, imprinting the fawns upon their mother.

The doe will keep her twin fawns near the birthing site for only a few hours before moving them to a more secure area. In the meantime, she remains attentive to details of cleansing the immediate area.

few hours, it may be several days before the newborn fawns become fully imprinted upon their mother. During the interim, the impressionable newborns risk being attracted to almost any large, moving object — even humans — which necessitates their early solitary existence.

FAWN HIDING BEHAVIOR

With regard to the mother-infant relationship shortly after birth, most ungulate species can be categorized as either "followers" or "hiders." These categorizations, actually differing adaptive strategies for protecting young from predation, tend to relate to the species' mobility and the prevailing habitat conditions.

Followers include such species as muskox and caribou, which are great travelers and live in open grassland or tundra. In these species, mother and young maintain close contact, communicate frequently, and the mothers actively defend the young from predators. The newborn must be strong and able to travel long distances when only a day or two old.

Hiders are species such as the white-tailed deer that occupy forested habitat, or relatively small species such as gazelles or antelope that can take advantage of low cover. Shortly after birth, mother and infant separate, except for brief periods of nursing and grooming, until

After her fawns are secured, fed, and resting, the doe pays attention to her own grooming, licking birth fluids from her hind quarters.

the young are old enough and strong enough to more effectively run from predators.

During its first six weeks of life, the fawn's chief defense against predators is to remain inactive and hide. Its speckled coat provides ideal camouflage, as it blends in perfectly with the spotted background of spring flora and the flecks of sunlight that filter through overhead foliage.

When undisturbed, the resting fawn holds its head up and is alert to potential danger. According to investigations conducted at Cornell University, the content fawn has an average heart rate of about 177 beats per minute (compared to 37 beats per minute for an adult) and breaths about 21 times per minute while resting. When frightened, however, the young fawn immediately drops its head, folds its ears back, assumes a curled or outstretched position, and instinctively "freezes." Its eyes remain open and its nose may quiver as it tests the air currents for an intruder's odors. But its heart rate drops to around 60 beats per minute, and breathing sometimes ceases altogether, a depressed physiological state referred to as "alarm bradycardia." Because many predators first detect their prey by its movements, the inactivity and alarm behavior demonstrated by fawns is probably an adaptation that further minimizes their chances of being found by a predator.

The general inactivity demonstrated by young fawns also allows for conservation of energy. Standing, walking, and running require extra energy that might be better used for growth, since rapid physical development is essential in becoming better equipped to escape from predators. Also, during its first month, the fawn's pelage offers minimal insulation because its guard hairs and underfur are not fully grown, resulting in excessive body heat loss when standing or active during inclement weather.

Although newborn fawns may spend about 95 percent of their time bedded, they occasionally stand, stretch, or shift bed sites if uncomfortable. If in an exposed location, they'll likely seek a shaded resting spot on a hot, sunny day, or may move to overhead cover during heavy rain. When less than two weeks old, fawns are generally active twice during daytime (when wolves and coyotes tend to be inactive) for about 10 to 30 minutes; fawns may also be active once, or not at all, at night. Although researcher's observations vary, I found that, unless disturbed, very young fawns seldom moved more than 50 feet without their mother's guidance.

While in the presence of their mothers, fawns less than a week old may exhibit bursts of running or play-type behavior — activity that is necessary for improving neuromuscular development and which occurs more

An hour-old fawn is uncoordinated and clumsy. Within hours, however, it will gain considerable strength and be capable of moving long distances under the direction of its mother.

frequently after two weeks of age. By the second week of life, fawns are active 10 to 15 percent of the time and are much more agile. By then they are also just as likely to run as to freeze when threatened.

MATERNAL CARE

The available literature is somewhat contradictory with regards to the maternal care exhibited by whitetail does during their fawns' early life. Apparently, strategies for predator defense vary somewhat from one region to another in order for does to cope with contrasting habitat conditions and effectively avoid predation of their young or themselves.

Despite their initially slow and wobbly demeanor, healthy newborn fawns are amazingly determined little critters. They are generally walking within 20 to 30 minutes after birth and are capable of traveling considerable distances when only a few hours old.

One of my investigations conducted in the Cusino enclosure involved the study of whitetail mother-infant relationships. While monitoring radio-collared deer, I learned that the doe's sudden sedentary behavior was a good clue that she had given birth to viable young. Such evidence then allowed me to intensively search a specific area for the fawns, and with good success.

In one instance my assistant Rod Clute came upon a doe that had just given birth to triplets. We waited about two hours before returning to the birth site and arrived just as the doe was about to move her fawns to new bedding locations. We then captured the fawns and equipped each with a radio-collar. When we relocated the fawns three hours later, one had moved 820 feet, one 755 feet, and the other 66 feet, demonstrating that, although they are typically hiders, healthy young fawns can be obedient followers capable of fairly long-distance movements through dense undergrowth when their mothers signal them that a "defensive move" is in order.

The doe nurses her fawn two or three times a day, and will lick the fawn's anal-genital area as it suckles. The licking behavior stimulates the fawn to defecate and urinate.

Although data are limited, it appears that most does stay with their fawns at the birth site for at least three hours. Following the initially critical period of cleansing, nursing, and imprinting, the mother then leads its young to widely spaced (100 to 400 feet apart) bed sites within her chosen fawning territory. The doe's "lead-follow" signals are not well documented by scientists but probably involve certain body posturing as well as soft, plaintive mewing and gentle nudging that encourage the young to follow. The advantage of spacing fawns is obvious: A predator might find and kill one fawn, but spacing of young fawns minimizes the chances that both or all three fawns would be lost. Siblings normally do not bed together until they are 18 to 32 days old, when they are physically capable of escaping predators. Those fawns that are malformed or too small and weak to leave the birth site, though, risk immediate abandonment.

The mother visits, grooms, and separately nurses her fawns only two or three times daily. Each fawn nurses (about eight ounces per meal) excitedly, its tail elevated and waggling, while standing transverse, head to tail, in relation to its mother's position. The mother's simultaneous grooming of the youngster's anal and genital areas stimulates the fawn to defecate and urinate at the nursing site. Such behavior, which may involve the mother's consuming of the urine and feces, minimizes odors that might attract predators; anal-genital licking generally ceases after the fawns are about two weeks old.

Some investigators suggest that the doe locates her fawns by odor, by approaching them upwind. Others suggest that the doe returns to the general vicinity where she left the fawns, then calls them with subtle mewing sounds. My observations indicate that both procedures are used but that calling is more commonly employed after the fawns are at least two weeks old.

Using electronic recording equipment and sophisticated sonograms, University of Georgia researchers led by Thomas Atkinson identified 12 different vocalizations made by white-tailed deer. Five of the vocalizations involved mothers and their young.

All deer "bawl" loudly when in situations of extreme stress, especially when injured or grasped. Except for nursing does, deer generally flee when hearing another deer bawl.

When approaching their fawn's bedding area, does commonly give out a "maternal grunt." This call, which is of low intensity and audible to humans for only a few yards, generally results in the fawn leaving its bed and running to the doe. If a fawn fails to respond, the doe often grunts more loudly.

Newborn fawns commonly "mew" in response to the doe's maternal grunt, or at other times when they seek maternal attention. Fawns also give out a louder "bleat," which seems to serve as a higher level of care soliciting, especially when the fawns are disturbed. When nursing, the content fawn often produces a brief, low-intensity "nursing whine."

Following each care session, the fawn is led from 200 to 400 feet to a fresh, odorless bed site. As a result, within relatively few days, the young fawn is introduced to its mother's fawning range, the boundaries of which are probably identifiably marked with the mother's odor through her urine or other sources. Thereafter, whenever disturbed or threatened by predators, the fawn flees, but not haphazardly; it stays within its familiar area, where maternal rescue is more likely.

The mother normally maintains an alert vigil while concealed in thick cover — a necessary component of favorable whitetail fawning habitat — usually within a few hundred feet of her resting fawn. If threatened, the distressed fawn's bawl brings mother running to the rescue within seconds. It's interesting to note, however, that the doe cannot readily distinguish the calls of her own fawns from those of strange individuals. Neither can she recognize them visually. Early in her fawn's life, its odor (possibly from the tarsal glands, located at the hock, on the inner surface of the hind legs) seems to be the only sure means of identification. Therefore, especially when doe fawning territories are closely aligned, it's not unusual to see two or sometimes even three does rush to defend a bawling fawn. Such behavior likely proves especially beneficial to the inexperienced young mother and her offspring, as the matriarch may on occasion lend some timely, albeit unintentional, defense against predators.

Oftentimes, even a strange fawn's distant distress call will cause a tentative doe to quickly check the well-being of her own offspring. If necessary, she will then relocate the young by leading them to the

An undisturbed fawn rests head up, alert for danger.

safety of dense cover. Sometimes, if one of her fawns falls victim to a predator and is obviously doomed, the mother behaves similarly, by immediately leading the surviving littermate to a more distant hiding place.

Does normally keep their fawns within the boundaries of their selected fawning territories during the first month after parturition. Sometimes, however, a serious predator threat may cause an older, highly dominant doe to lead her young to a temporary new location as much as a half mile outside her usual fawning grounds, but within the ancestral range. Young does seem less likely to exhibit such behavior, possibly because they are not so maternally motivated or because their subordinate social rank prevents them from trespassing upon the fawning territories of older does.

The displaced mother and her fawns usually return to their normal range within a few days, presumably once the threat of predation passes. In one such instance, however, I observed the doe to position her fawn on an island within a broad shallow stream, where it remained for an entire week before resuming more normal movement patterns.

As noted previously, in the savanna grasslands of Texas, does with newborn behave differently: They commonly leave their young in hiding while they themselves graze with other deer. Hirth observed, for example, that

"in its first few days, a fawn begins to select a bedding spot away from its mother and to move its hiding place frequently. Observations indicate that after nursing, a fawn walks some 15 to 30 yards from its mother to a bedding site in dense cover. The doe seems to pay no attention to the fawn's departure or to the location of the bedding place. By picking its own spot and changing it frequently, the fawn avoids having its mother's scent associated with its hiding place."

Contrary to Hirth's studies, newborn fawns I studied in northern Michigan were highly dependent upon their mothers for guidance. Although very young fawns likely selected the exact location where they bedded, the mother determined the fawn's movement patterns. Regardless of the mother's age, those fawns I handled or disturbed traveled two to three times farther before rebedding when accompanied by the mother than when moving alone.

Without question, maternally experienced does, generally those four or more years old, make the best mothers; they display superior maternal behavior traits that differ from those of younger mothers. Compared to first-time mothers, prime-aged does in my studies maintained smaller home ranges, probably because the older mothers were more dominant and able to hold superior habitat. The fawns of older does also occupied smaller ranges, siblings were spaced farther apart, and were moved greater distances between consecutive daytime bedding sites during their first two weeks, as compared to fawns of younger mothers.

When faced with predation by black bears, these behavioral differences associated with maternal experience and learning paid great dividends, as the older does lost only 17 percent of their fawns, while first-time and second-time mothers lost 58 and 32 percent of their fawns, respectively. Experienced mothers rarely lost single fawns or both members of twin litters, whereas complete litter failure among young does was not uncommon.

Prime-aged does even responded defensively to artificially induced predator odor. When I placed coyote urine in the vicinity of their

bedded, radio-transmitter-equipped fawns, studies showed older does moved their young about twice as far as they would in a normal move from one bed site to the next. But such treatment had no obvious effect upon the behavior of younger does and their fawns.

Among the maternal care strategies employed by whitetail does, outright defense of their young fawns against predators may be as important as any single factor influencing fawn survival. Irate does have been known to charge and strike at coyotes and domestic dogs, and even humans, in defense of their fawns. But such behavior is more commonly displayed by healthy, maternally experienced does. Given a serious predator threat, a malnourished or young mother is more likely to flee from the scene.

Older does are the most successful mothers. Their prior experience raising fawns makes them more protective of their young, and their caregiving strategies are better developed than those of young does.

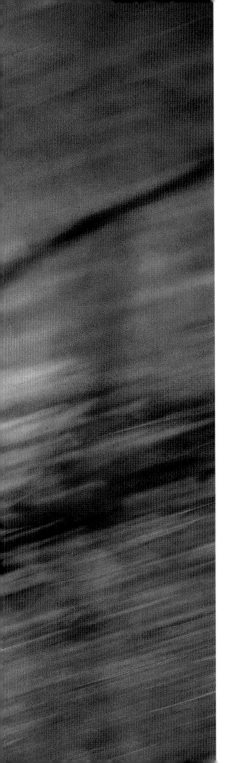

FAWN MORTALITY

Most animals characteristically produce more young than can be expected to survive. White-tailed deer are no exception. Although the reasons vary from one region to another, a high proportion of the whitetail fawns born each spring fail to survive their first few weeks.

Typically, fawns born in areas of high-quality habitat where deer numbers are maintained below carrying capacity of the range through adequate hunter harvest have the best chances of surviving early life. For example, more than 90 percent of the fawns born on rich farmlands in portions of the Midwest survive to weaning age. Conversely, infant mortality rates ranging from 50 to 90 percent often prevail in poor-quality habitat where food and cover are inadequate, in northern areas following particularly severe winters, or wherever deer are overly abundant.

Between the ages of two weeks and two months, fawns increase activities independent of their mothers. Still too slow to escape predators, many fawns succumb to coyotes, wolves, and domestic dogs.

NUTRITION

Since deer on northern range commonly experience a negative energy balance during winter while subsisting on a diet of woody browse, pregnant does must catabolize (burn) fat deposits to make up for the energy deficit. If the doe's diet is inadequate and especially low in protein, she will draw upon her bone and body tissues to nourish the fetuses she carries. Prolonged nutritional deprivation during harsh winters often contributes to poor fetal growth and sometimes results in the death of the unborn, if not that of the mother too.

The fawn's size at birth will hinge upon the mother's nutritional status during the final trimester of pregnancy, and the fawn's birth weight will largely determine its prospects for surviving its first few days. Healthy whitetail fawns normally weigh from six to nine pounds at birth, but some may weigh as much as 12 pounds, with southern subspecies birthing somewhat smaller.

Investigations conducted by Lou Verme at the Cusino Wildlife Research Station revealed that over 90 percent of the offspring born to pen-confined does that were malnourished throughout pregnancy died shortly after birth. In contrast, roughly 95 percent of those born to well-fed mothers survived. Survivors, on average, weighed about eight pounds, whereas those that died weighed about four pounds at birth. Based on this research, fawns weighing less than five pounds at birth appear to have relatively slim chances of surviving more than a couple of days, regardless of other favorable circumstances.

Verme's investigations revealed that malnourished does rarely absorbed or aborted fetuses, but that stillbirths of full-term fawns were quite common. In some cases even dead, mummified fetuses were carried to term. Most fawns were born alive but were stunted in size and perished within a day or two. These fawns were either too weak to stand or too small to nurse, or were born to mothers that produced no milk.

Nutritional shortage early in gestation tends to impact the growth of twin fetuses about equally. During the last third of their development, however, serious diet deficiency often results in physical dimorphism, wherein one littermate receives a greater share of the limited sustenance that is available. Consequently, does poorly nourished during late pregnancy tend to produce fawns that differ greatly in body size. When that is the case, the smaller fawn's prospects for survival, almost invariably, are not good.

Outright starvation losses of deer on northern range can be sizeable during particularly severe winters. Depending upon the magnitude of winter severity, total newborn fawn losses may be staggering. In all

Fawns born to well-nourished does stand the best chances of survival. The fawn's birth weight will largely determine its prospects of surviving its first few days of life.

Abandonment by the doe means certain death for young fawns.
Without maternal care, they will die of starvation or predation
within a matter of days.

likelihood, serious fawning losses occur throughout northern deer range after hard winters. Records compiled at the Cusino Wildlife Research Station during the late 1960s and early 1970s revealed that newborn fawn losses in Upper Michigan varied from only 10 percent after mild winters to as much as 75 percent following a severe one.

"As we might expect," related Verme, "natal mortality was lowest following mild winters, with the rate rising sharply as weather severity increased. We found that fawning deaths were greatest when deer were forced to yard up early in the winter and could not leave the swamps until mid-April. Faced with a prolonged siege of hunger plus deep snow and bitter cold, the pregnant doe eventually 'runs out of gas,' and the odds against the fawn's survival at birth literally skyrockets. Nutritional stress is, of course, most ravaging to yearling does bearing their first young, and to older mothers. Even does in the prime of life carrying twins or triplets are not immune, however; one or more of their fawns may be hopelessly stunted from malnutrition."

Compared with cow's milk, deer milk is richer in fat, protein, dry solids, and energy. Given a good milk supply, fawns usually double their birth weight in about two weeks and triple it within a month. On average, well-nourished fawns gain nearly one-half pound per day during this period. Single fawns normally gain weight faster than do twins or triplets, probably because the single fawn consumes more milk per feeding.

If the doe receives insufficient nutrition to support normal milk production, the milk remains of uniformly high quality but the total amount produced tends to decline. Hence, a doe living on poor range might produce a limited supply of milk and ultimately raise relatively small fawns because of it. In such a case, twins or triplets would pose an especially heavy burden. On the other hand, if the mother's diet was severely restricted, as might sometimes occur on poor quality southern range during times of severe drought or during severe spring flooding, the doe might produce no milk at all. In that event, if her fawns were very young and without functional rumen development, they would die from starvation.

ABANDONMENT

Whitetail does normally make good mothers. Abandonment of newborn fawns is most commonly associated with malnutrition, especially during late pregnancy, and occurs most frequently among first-time mothers. Even when disturbed during the critical period shortly after giving birth, maternally experienced does tend to prevail, imprint upon their fawns, and defend

Fawns born below optimal birth weight, or born to malnourished mothers, may be abandoned at birth or shortly thereafter.

their young as best they can. Young does producing their first young, however, are more apt to abandon their young when threatened, in favor of saving themselves.

One of the most comprehensive studies of the effects of winter nutritional stress on maternal care traits of white-tailed deer was conducted by Ed Langenau and John Lerg at the Houghton Lake Wildlife Research Station, located in central Lower Michigan. In their study, 27 percent of the does on low quality winter diets abandoned their fawns, versus only two percent abandonment for well-nourished does. The most common form of newborn fawn mortality within a few days after birth resulted from a "maternal rejection syndrome."

According to Langenau and Lerg, "Does which failed to nurse or care for their young displayed fear and aggressive postures toward fawns, birth fluids, and afterbirth. This lack of an initial mother-young bond caused the fawns to increase the amount of care-soliciting behaviors such as bleating, running at the doe, and time out of the bed. This response of the fawns probably reinforced the fear and aggressive behavior in the doe." In Langenau's and Lerg's study, the lack of an initial doe-fawn bond was confirmed to be critical to fawn survival. Without the important bond, fawns never nursed, and died within 77 hours after birth. In the case of twins, both were usually abandoned.

This phenomenon of fawn rejection by malnourished mothers is similar to that resulting from cases of high deer density and crowding, wherein psychologically stressed first-time mothers abandon otherwise healthy offspring because they cannot find solitude and fawn-rearing space. In either case, such abnormal behavior likely arises because of an insufficient production of prolactin, a hormone produced by the pituitary gland and which induces milk secretion and promotes the maternal instinct.

Although captive nursing does sometimes adopt orphaned fawns, I know of no such observations for wild whitetails. In the wild, abandoned fawns either die from starvation within a couple of days after birth or are killed by predators alerted to their bawling. One can generally surmise that a young fawn walking about on its own, bawling, is in deep trouble. Most likely, such an individual has been orphaned and is nearing death from starvation.

ACCIDENTS

Infant whitetails tend to be obedient creatures highly dependent upon their mother's guidance and protection. But even in their mother's presence they are ungainly and highly susceptible to injury and accidental death. During their first few days, many newborn fawns die when they become entangled in fences, stranded in mud holes, drown, or incur any of a host of accidents that befall inquisitive and ungainly young of the forest.

On average, even well fed whitetail does living on excellent deer range lose about 10 percent of their fawns as the result of birth defects and accidents. The accidental death rate of newborn fawns will be highest, however, where deer density is high and where surplus mothers must attempt to raise fawns in mediocre or outright dangerous fawn-rearing habitat.

Before the advent of flushing bars and other special mechanical devices designed to flush fawns ahead of

Accidents, including car-deer collisions, take a toll on the annual fawn crop, especially where high deer densities occur in populated areas.

farm machinery, mowing machines accounted for the death of many fawns that lay hidden in hay fields. Today, highway accidents may take a heavy toll of fawns in certain areas. Since the mother often encourages the fawn to flatten and hide when threatened, the startled fawn might crouch and attempt to hide just about anywhere, even on a busy highway. (I recall examining a fawn brought to me that had been accidentally killed by its mother. When surprised by a vehicle approaching along a forested roadway, the mother, in attempting to make its fawn crouch and hide, struck it with her hoof, breaking the fawn's neck and killing it instantly.) Fawns also fall from steep cliffs or embankments, impediments that normally pose only minor obstacles to their agile mothers.

Drowning probably claims as many young fawns as any type of accident, possibly because dense vegetation along stream banks and lake shorelines makes ideal hiding cover for fawns. Even

though young fawns might be capable of swimming short distances, they often are unable to scale steep stream banks, and mothers sometimes attempt to lead small fawns across torrential streams, steep drainage ditches, or large bodies of deep water that adult deer traverse easily, but which prove fatal to wobbly fawns. Flooding may also claim many newborn fawns.

DISEASE AND PARASITES

Disease and parasitism seldom pose a serious threat to well nourished newborn fawns on northern range. In the South, however, bacterial diseases, screwworm flies, stomach worms, lung worms, ticks, and assorted other infections periodically cause serious problems for whitetails. Regardless of the region or the environment, such maladies will be most prevalent among malnourished whitetails living in high density populations.

Although viral diseases in whitetails are poorly understood and most occur infrequently, some are profoundly

Birth defects also affect fawn survival. This fawn, born with a dry socket, may live with sight in only one eye, but it will be especially susceptible to accidents and predation.

pathogenic to deer, and certain ones are known to reduce newborn fawn survival rates. Mucosal disease, for example, which is usually spread through ingestion of contaminated food or water or via inhalation of the virus, may also be transmitted from the pregnant female to the fetus. Abortions, stillbirths, and newborn fawn mortality were observed among pregnant whitetails experimentally infected with the disease, but the potential of this disease for wild deer populations is unknown.

Salmonellosis infections spawned by the bacterium *Salmonella* may cause heavy mortality among newborn fawns raised in captivity. But salmonellosis may occur wherever a favorable microhabitat exists. The disease occurs almost exclusively in young fawns and has occasionally caused severe die-offs of fawns in certain parts of Texas.

Salmonellosis is acquired most commonly by ingestion of contaminated food or water, or possibly shortly after birth in association with amniotic fluids. In Texas, the infection was restricted primarily to the floodplains of moist river bottoms. Other investigations also revealed the *Salmonella* organism in alluvial sediments, supporting the contention that salmonellosis occurs most frequently in environments subject to periodic flooding.

In very young fawns, *Salmonella* infection may spread rapidly through the bloodstream, resulting in death without symptoms of diarrhea. Generally, the sick fawn fails to groom itself, leading to ruffled hair and an unkempt appearance. Dehydration causes the skin about the face to tighten, the eyes to appear sunken, and rapidly weakens the animal. Once the animal becomes severely dehydrated, it is unable to stand and usually dies within a few hours. In more-disease-resistant fawns — those generally a few weeks old — diarrhea generally develops within 12 to 24 hours following infection. Affected fawns become weakened and reluctant to move but usually are able to stand. Also, convulsive seizures due to an electrolyte imbalance generally develop. In the wild, such infected fawns are generally found dead.

Whitetails harbor a variety of external and internal parasites, including certain protozoa, worms (helminths), and arthropod pests such as ticks and lice. Only the helminths, of which 35 species have been identified in whitetails living in the southeastern United States, seem to pose a significant threat to the health of adult whitetails.

Little reference can be found in the literature relative to the occurrence of protozoan parasites in newborn whitetails. Some investigators speculate, however, that parasitic infections could lead to abortions or to various neurological problems fatal to newborn fawns. That

speculation is based on the fact that certain parasitic organisms carried by a pregnant doe can cross to fetal membranes and invade fetal tissues.

Many of the larger parasitic worms, including lung worms and stomach worms, may prove fatal to fawns that are several months old. Because most such parasites require considerable time to develop once contracted, they probably do not cause immediate problems in very young fawns. However, the threadworm (*Strongyloides papillosus*) — which produces the disease referred to as strongyloidosis — can be fatal to very young fawns. This parasite is usually found in the small intestine, and infestation results in death within 12 to 36 hours after onset of its primary symptom, diarrhea. In addition to becoming infected through ingestion of the parasite's larvae with food or water, newborn fawns may acquire the parasite via colostrum or milk, or be infected in the fetal stage by the mother. Serious infections may develop in prenatally infected fawns in as few as five days after birth. One serious outbreak of strongyloidosis in a captive deer herd in Florida killed 39 percent of the fawns born in the herd over a nine-year period.

Prior to effective screwworm fly (*Callitroga hominivorax*) eradication programs initiated in 1958 and 1962, the screwworm fly was the most important arthropod pest of white-tailed deer in the southern United States. Since then, screwworm infestations have largely been controlled in the United States, although outbreaks still occur in Latin America and occasionally in Mexico and Texas.

In order to complete its life cycle, the female screwworm fly must deposit her eggs in an open wound on a live, warm-blooded animal. The resultant larvae then feed on tissues of the infected animal, producing serious damage and secondary infection. The flies often deposit eggs on the umbilical cord of newborn fawns; the larvae then enter the body cavity and ultimately kill the

Drowning is a common mortality factor among fawns. Does often lead their young to or across water courses that prove to be death traps for the young deer.

infected fawn. During years of heavy screwworm infestation, up to 80 percent of the fawn crop on the King Ranch in Texas are known to have died from screwworm-induced mortality.

Today, ticks are probably the most important ectoparasite infecting white-tailed deer in North America. About 18 species of ticks have been found on whitetails, 13 of which are relatively common. Aside from causing severe blood loss and providing wounds for secondary infections, and sometimes even causing blindness in young fawns, blood-sucking ticks transmit certain diseases.

The lone-star tick (*Amblyomma americanum*), in particular, has been implicated in heavy mortality of newborn fawns in eastern Oklahoma. Investigators led by John Bolte reported newborn fawns literally covered with larvae, nymphs, and adult stages of the tick at the Cookson Hill Wildlife Refuge. In 1968, tick bites and gross tissue damage around the eyes and head, in particular, led to secondary infections, contributing to blindness and death of 34 percent of the newborn fawns on the area.

PREDATION

Just about every meat-eater in the whitetail's range feeds upon deer when the opportunity arises. Certainly,

not all of these carnivores can be considered effective predators of newborn whitetails — some are, but others function strictly as scavengers.

Young whitetails are well endowed with inherited antipredator strategies that help minimize their detection and increase their chances of surviving early life. Still, fawns are lost to various predators, but the extent to which predation is expedited by disease obscures the number of deaths caused solely by predators. The effects of disease and parasitism are especially difficult to separate from those of predation because disease-stricken and

A litter of coyotes awaits the return of mother and a meal—possibly the flesh of a whitetail fawn.

parasite-loaded fawns are less likely to escape from predators once detected. Also, sick fawns frequently have diarrhea or produce mucous secretions, the odors of which may attract sharp-nosed predators.

Likewise, throughout the white-tails range, small fawns weakened by malnutrition become more vulnerable to predators, especially if they or their mothers exhibit maladaptive behaviors. Therefore, given the presence of alert preda-tors and opportunistic scavengers, and based upon the few scattered fragments of evidence usually discovered near its carcass, deter-mining the primary cause of a young fawn's death may not be an easy matter.

Predation involving any species generally centers on the doomed surpluses of the prey population. But, according to the distinguished ecologist Paul Errington, "The victims of predation need not be manifestly unfit. Insecurity of position can impose as deadly a handicap on an animal in normal

physical condition as can the sluggishness or weakness of an animal that is physically subnormal." In species like white-tailed deer, then, learning, social behavior, and intense competition for favorable habitat also become important fac-tors determining whether a doe's newborn fawns might fall victim to predators.

An overabundance of whitetails and the resultant overutilization of their range can lead to a reduction in both nutritious foods and fawn hiding cover, thereby improving predator hunting success. In addi-tion, because fawn-rearing does are territorial, a spill-over of surplus does into unsuitable fawn-rearing habitat when deer density is high yields newborn fawns exceptionally vulnerable to predation.

The most important predators of newborn fawns include gray wolves, mountain lions, coyotes, black bears, bobcats, and domestic dogs. In special cases, however, red foxes, fishers, lynx, and even birds of prey such as golden eagles, bald eagles, and ravens might kill

Domestic dogs kill large numbers of deer every year. Commonly, they hamstring an animal, then leave it to die.

fawns weakened from malnutrition, abandonment, parasites, or disease.

Coyotes are important predators of newborn fawns, especially in semiarid portions of the Southwest lacking protective hiding cover. Studies conducted on the Welder Wildlife Refuge on the plains of south Texas revealed that, annually, 72 percent of the whitetail fawns died, and 93 percent of those deaths occurred in the first month after fawn birth. Even higher losses of newborn whitetails were reported from the Wichita Mountains of Oklahoma. Although accidents, parasites, and disease were implicated in the death of some fawns, predation by coyotes accounted for more than half of the mortality in the Texas study and nearly all of the fawn mortality in the Oklahoma area.

Similar findings were reported by Texas Parks and Wildlife Department researchers Bob Carroll and Dennis Brown in the lower Post Oak Savannah area of southern Texas. The investigators reported that annual fawn mortality rates varied appreciably, however, depending upon the amount of rainfall, which in turn determined the quality and availability of deer foods and fawn hiding cover during spring and early summer. Fawn losses ranged from 10 percent during years of heavy rainfall to as much as 90 percent during years of drought. Overall, about half of the fawns died because of disease, starvation, and predation; half of the loss was attributed to predation by coyotes.

Samuel Beasom of Texas A&M University studied the impact of predation on the productivity of whitetails in south Texas by removing coyotes and bobcats from one area and comparing the results to a control area. Over a two-year period, fawns were about twice as abundant on the area where predators were removed. Coyote reduction on Fort Sill, Oklahoma, also resulted in a substantial increase in newborn fawn survival. Beasom concluded: "It seems probable that white-tailed deer densities could be increased [in south Texas] with intensive predator control efforts if other compensating sources of mortality did not become immediately operative. However, it would be unwise to attempt this under a program of light hunter harvesting without a longer term research project to see how high deer density would go before being stabilized by some other factors."

Some investigators propose that coyotes have developed a specialization for preying upon whitetail fawns in open habitat, as occurs in the brush country of south Texas and the prairies of Oklahoma. Since coyotes hunt primarily by sight, researchers speculate that those living in open habitat are able to watch does return to nurse fawns, thereby learning the fawn's hiding place.

Coyotes appear to be far less successful in finding

Coyotes rarely prey on healthy adult deer but often follow wolves to scavenge the remains of their kills.

newborn fawns in the dense ground cover that prevails throughout most of the Midwest, Great Lakes region, and the Northeast. No predation occurred among 33 radio-collared fawns in Minnesota, and only two percent loss due to predation was recorded in a central Missouri study. Domestic dogs killed eight percent of the fawns in a study conducted in the Missouri Ozarks. In south-central Iowa and southern Illinois, coyotes and domestic dogs killed an estimated 21 percent and 20 percent, respectively, of the annual fawn crops.

Thomas Nelson and Alan Woolf of Southern Illinois University studied newborn fawn mortality on the Crab Orchard National Wildlife Refuge in southern Illinois. They reported that summer mortality rates for 54 radio-collared fawns averaged 30 percent. Coyotes and domestic dogs accounted for 69 percent of the natural mortalities, and most of the fawns killed were 27 to 47 days old.

The Illinois researchers concluded: "Predation showed a rather direct relationship to fawn activity levels, and perhaps more importantly to increased independent activity. Fawns less than two weeks old were well protected from predators by their cryptic color and inactivity; fawns greater than eight weeks old were generally too swift to be caught by canids. However, there was a vulnerability during the transition period, when

Although not a serious threat to fully grown, healthy whitetails, coyotes can easily dispatch a hapless fawn.

In spring, black bears wander over large areas in search of food. When whitetails occupy the same area as bears, fawns commonly become part of the ursine diet.

fawns were more active and observable but still catchable." Such logic may apply equally well to most forest-dominated areas characterized by dense undergrowth.

There is ample, well-documented evidence that in certain areas black bears are important predators of newborn whitetails, elk, and moose. Canadian researchers suggest that such easily digested animal protein becomes an important "or even necessary" part of the bear's diet in spring, before berries and mast become available.

Black bears proved to be effective predators of newborn whitetails when they unexpectedly entered the Cusino deer enclosure during the spring period. Given that the enclosed deer were supplementally fed and in excellent health year-round when held at moderate density, they were extremely productive. Annually, under normal conditions, only about 10 percent of the newborn fawns died, primarily from birth defects, stillbirths, or accidents. However, during years when bears were present, average newborn fawn mortality rates increased to 32 percent. Radio-tracking studies of does and their fawns verified that the increased losses were due to bear predation and, in all cases, the fawns killed were less than one month old.

In my studies, bears annually killed about 22 percent of the available fawns. However, young does suffered dis-

proportionately greater losses than did older does. Prime-aged does lost only slightly more fawns when bears were present versus absent. However, two- and three-year-old mothers suffered heavy fawn mortality when bears were present. Experienced does rarely lost single fawns or both members of twin litters, whereas complete litter failure among young does was not uncommon. Although maternally-experienced does occupied superior fawn-rearing habitat, I concluded that learning experience and outright defense of their young largely accounted for the older doe's improved

fawn-rearing success when threatened by bears.

The gray wolf likely played a key role in the evolutionary development of antipredator strategies in whitetails. Tests conducted by Aaron Moen and coworkers at Cornell University revealed that even very young fawns possess an innate fear of wolves, based upon their response to wolf howls. In special tests, the Cornell researchers found that fawns less than seven weeks old exhibited alarm bradycardia in response to recorded wolf howls, but older fawns exhibited both increases and decreases in heart rate. Therefore, the pattern of responses recorded generally matched the fawns' physical development and ability to escape predators.

Even where they coexist today, newborn fawns are an important item in the diet of wolves. In northern Minnesota, for example, researchers found evidence of white-tailed deer in more than 80 percent of wolf scats examined from mid-June to mid-July, and nearly half of the deer remains detected were those of fawns.

In their Minnesota study, biologists David Mech and Ronald McRoberts concluded that where whitetails live in the presence of wolves, fawn survival varies according to maternal age. That is, as in my findings involving black bear predation, when threatened by wolves, older female whitetails were better able to protect and defend their fawns from predation.

Generally, the bobcat is not considered to be an important predator of newborn whitetails. Although they have been identified as important predators of newborn pronghorn antelope (killing 40 percent of the tagged animals in a Utah study), studies conducted in the South indicate that bobcats are far less effective than coyotes in killing young whitetails.

Now extirpated from most of its former range in eastern North America, the mountain lion also likely played an important role in the evolutionary development of antipredator strategies in whitetails, especially as related

Wherever gray wolves and whitetails coexist, the deer are a primary food source of these large predators. In spring, fawns may suffer considerable mortality from marauding wolf packs.

Despite the many dangers they face from malnutrition, accidents, disease, and predation, some fawns will always survive and bring about new generations of white-tailed deer.

to the rearing of fawns. Although data are lacking for whitetails, newborn mule deer in the West tend to represent a large part of the mountain lion's spring and summer diet. Historically, newborn whitetails probably did too, and probably do today wherever the two species coexist.

THE SURVIVORS

When provided with favorable habitat, white-tailed deer are geared for maximum reproduction. Many environmental constraints interact, however, to determine how many fawns will be born and how many will survive to weaning age.

Even under the most ideal circumstances, some newborn fawns die due to natural causes. And in the presence of effective predators such as gray wolves, mountain lions, black bears, coyotes, or bobcats, a 20 to 30 percent loss can be expected, even among well-nourished deer living in optimal habitat. Healthy deer populations can easily absorb such loss. In fact, such a drain helps to dampen wild oscillations in deer population size, thereby protecting the habitat from overuse. Most importantly, the selective culling by predators functions to remove fawns with inferior physical and behavioral characteristics that would be harmful to the species if perpetuated.

On the other hand, most of the newborn fawns might die during some years in areas where deer are overly abundant. Too many deer causes undue stress and opens the door for disease and parasites. Also, overuse of habitat by deer reduces the availability of preferred foods, devastates fawn-rearing habitat, and contributes to malnutrition. Obviously, then, in the absence of effective natural predators — without proper deer population control through regulated harvesting by human predators — the whitetail can become its own worst enemy.

Most of the time, even under the most dismal spring conditions, some infant whitetails will survive. Those survivors, the products of natural selection, will be the hardiest of their kind. Given good nutrition, they will grow rapidly during summer, changing from fragile infants dependent upon their mother's milk to robust ruminants capable of fending for themselves. Whitetail summer will not be without its perils for this new generation of deer. The environmental pressures operating then, however, will be relatively weak in comparison to the harsh forces that prevailed in the critical period of time we call whitetail spring.

SELECTED REFERENCES

Armstrong, R. A. 1950. Fetal development of the northern white-tailed deer (*Odocoileus virginianus borealis* Miller). *Amer. Midland Nat.* 43: 650-666.

Atkeson, T. D., R. L. Marchinton, and K. V. Miller. 1988. Vocalizations of white-tailed deer. *Amer. Midland Nat.* 120: 194-200.

Beasom, S. L. 1974. Relationships between predator removal and white-tailed deer net productivity. *J. Wildlife Mgmt.* 38: 854-859.

Bolte, J. R., J. A. Hair, and J. Fletcher. 1970. White-tailed deer mortality following tissue destruction induced by lone star ticks. *J. Wildlife Mgmt.* 34: 546-552.

Brown, B. A., Jr. 1974. Social organization in male groups of white-tailed deer. in *The behaviour of ungulates and its relation to management*, ed. V. Geist and F. Walther, pp. 436-446. 2 vol. New Series Publ. 24. Morges, Switzerland: IUCN. 940 pp.

Brown, R. D., ed. 1983. *Antler development in Cervidae.* Caesar Kleberg Wildl. Res. Inst., Kingsville, TX. 480 pp.

Bubenik, G. A., and A. B. Bubenik, eds. 1990. *Horns, pronghorns, and antlers: evolution, morphology, physiology, and social significance.* Springer-Verlag New York Inc., 562 pp.

Carroll, B. K., and D. L. Brown. 1977. Factors affecting neonatal fawn survival in south-central Texas. *J. Wildlife Mgmt.* 41: 63-69.

Cook, R. S., M. White, D. O. Trainer, and W. C. Glazener. 1971. Radio-telemetry for fawn mortality studies. *Wildl. Dis. Assoc. Bull.* 3:160-165.

Cook, R. S., M. White, D. O. Trainer, and W. C. Glazener. 1967. Mortality of young white-tailed deer fawns in South Texas. *J. Wildlife Mgmt.* 35: 47-56.

Crawford, H. S. 1982. Seasonal food selection and digestibility by tame white-tailed deer in central Maine. *J. Wildlife Mgmt.* 46: 974-982.

Dasman, W. 1971. *If deer are to survive.* Stackpole Books. Harrisburg, PA. 128 pp.

Davison, W. R., F. A. Hayes, V. F. Nettles, and F. E. Kellogg, eds. 1981. *Diseases and parasites of white-tailed deer.* Tallahassee, FLa.: Tall Timbers Research Station. 458 pp.

Downing, R. L., and B. S. McGinnes. 1969. Capturing and marking white-tailed deer fawns. *J. Wildlife Mgmt.* 33: 711-714.

Garner, G. W., and J. A. Morrison. 1980. Observations of interspecific behavior between predators and white-tailed in southwestern Oklahoma. *J. Mammal.* 61: 126-130.

Gerlach, D., S. Atwater, and J. Schnell (Eds.). 1994. *Deer.* Stackpole Books. Mechanicsburg, PA. 384 pp.

Goss, R. J. 1983. *Deer antlers: regeneration, function, and evolution.* Academic Press, NY. 316 pp.

Halls, L. K., ed. 1984. *White-tailed deer: ecology and management.* Wildl. Manage. Inst., The Stackpole Co., Harrisburg, PA. 870 pp.

Haugen, A. O. 1975. Reproductive performance of white-tailed deer in Iowa. *J. Mammal.* 56: 151-159.

Haugen, A. O., and D. W. Speake. 1958. Determining age of young fawn white-tailed deer. *J. Wildlife Mgmt.* 22: 319-321.

Hawkins, R. E., and W. D. Klimstra. 1970. A preliminary study of social organization of white-tailed deer. *J. Wildlife Mgmt.* 34: 407-419.

Hirth, D. H. 1977. Social behavior of white-tailed deer in relation to habitat. *Wildl. Monogr.* 53. 55 pp.

Hoffman, R. A., and P. R. Robinson. 1966. Changes in some endocrine glands of white-tailed deer as affected by season, sex and age. *J. Mammal.* 47: 266-280.

Huegel, C. N., R. B. Dahlgren, and H. L. Gladfelter. 1985. Mortality of white-tailed deer fawns in south-central Iowa. *J. Wildlife Mgmt.* 49:377-380.

Huegel, C. N., R. B. Dahlgren, and H. L. Gladfelter. 1985. Use of doe behavior to capture white-tailed deer fawns. *Wildl. Soc. Bull.* 13: 287-289.

Jackson, R. M., M. White, and F. F. Knowlton. 1972. Activity patterns of young white-tailed deer fawns in south Texas. *Ecology* 53: 262-270.

Jacobsen, N. K. 1979. Alarm bradycardia in white-tailed deer fawns (*Odocoileus virginianus*). *J. Mammal.* 60: 343-349.

Jacobsen, N. K. 1984. Changes in 24-hour activity patterns with growth of white-tailed deer fawns (*Odocoileus virginianus*). *J. Interdiscipl. Cycle Res.* 15: 213-226.

Langenau, E. E., Jr., and J. M. Lerg. 1976. The effects of winter nutritional stress on maternal and neonatal behavior in penned white-tailed deer. *Appl. Animal Ethology* 2: 207-223.

Lent, P. C. 1974. Mother-infant relationships in ungulates. in *The behavior of ungulates and its relation to management.* ed. V. Geist and F. Walther, pp. 14-55. 1 vol. New Series Publ. 24. Morges, Switzerland: IUCN. 940 pp.

McCullough, D. R. 1979. *The George Reserve deer herd: population ecology of a K-selected species.* Ann Arbor: Univ. Michigan Press. 271 pp.

McGinnes, B. S., and R. L. Downing. 1977. Factors affecting the peak of white-tailed deer fawning in Virginia. *J. Wildlife Mgmt.* 41: 715-719.

Mech, L. D., and R. E. McRoberts. 1990. Survival of white-tailed deer fawns in relation to maternal age. *J. Mammal.* 71: 465-467.

Melchiors, M. A., and C. A. Leslie. 1985. Effectiveness of predator fecal odors as black-tailed deer repellents. *J. Wildlife Mgmt.* 49: 358-362.

Michael, E. D. 1964. Birth of white-tailed deer fawns. *J. Wildlife Mgmt.* 28:171-173.

Mirarchi, R. E., P. F. Scanlon, R. L. Kirkpatrick, and C. B. Schreck. 1977. Androgen levels and antler development in captive and wild white-tailed deer. *J. Wildlife Mgmt.* 41: 178-183.

Moen, A. N., M. A. DellaFerra, A. L. Hiller, and B. A. Buxton. 1978. Heart rates of white-tailed deer fawns in response to recorded wolf howls. *Canadian J. Zool.* 56:1207-1210.

Nelson, M. E., and L. D. Mech. 1992. Dispersal in female white-tailed deer. *J. Mammal.* 73: 891-894.

Nelson, T. A., and A. Woolf. 1987. Mortality of white-tailed deer fawns in southern Illinois. *J. Wildlife Mgmt.* 51: 326-329.

Nixon, C. M., L. P. Hansen, P. A. Brewer, and J. E. Chelsvig. 1991. Ecology of white-tailed deer in an intensively farmed region of Illinois. *Wildl. Monog.* 118. Washington D. C.: The Wildlife Society. 77 pp.

Nixon, C. M., L. P. Hansen, P. A. Brewer, and J. E. Chelsvig. 1992. Stability of white-tailed doe parturition ranges in east-central Illinois. *Can. J. Zool.* 70: 968-973.

O'Pezio, J. P. 1978. Mortality among white-tailed deer fawns on the Seneca Army Depot. *N. Y. Fish and Game J.* 25: 1-15.

Ozoga, J. J., and L. J. Verme. 1978. The thymus gland as a nutritional status indicator in deer. *J. Wildlife Mgmt.* 42: 791-798.

Ozoga, J. J., and L. J. Verme. 1982. Physical and reproductive characteristics of a supplementally-fed white-tailed deer herd. *J. Wildlife Mgmt.* 46: 281-301.

Ozoga, J. J., and L. J. Verme. 1982. Predation by black bears on newborn white-tailed deer. *J. Mammal.* 63: 695-696.

Ozoga, J. J., L. J. Verme, and C. S. Bienz. 1982. Parturition behavior and territoriality in white-tailed deer: impact on neonatal mortality. *J. Wildlife Mgmt.* 46: 1-ll.

Ozoga, J. J., C. S. Bienz, and L. J. Verme. 1982. Red fox feeding habits in relation to fawn mortality. *J. Wildlife Mgmt.* 46: 242-243.

Ozoga, J. J., and L. J. Verme. 1984. Effects of family-bond deprivation on reproductive performance in female white-tailed deer. *J. Wildlife Mgmt.* 48: 1326-1334.

Ozoga, J. J., and L. J. Verme. 1985. Determining fetus age in live white-tailed does by x-ray. *J. Wildlife Mgmt.* 49: 372-374.

Ozoga, J. J., and L. J. Verme. 1986. Initial and subsequent maternal success of white-tailed deer. *J. Wildlife Mgmt.* 50:122-124.

Ozoga, J. J., and L. J. Verme. 1986. Relation of maternal age to fawn-rearing success in white-tailed deer. *J. Wildlife Mgmt.* 50: 480-486.

Ozoga, J. J. 1987. Maximum fecundity in supplementally fed northern Michigan white-tailed deer. *J. Wildlife Mgmt.* 68: 878-879.

Ozoga, J. J., and R. K. Clute. 1988. Mortality rates of marked and unmarked fawns. *J. Wildlife Mgmt.* 52: 549-551.

Palmer, R. S. 1951. The white-tailed deer of Tomhegan Camps, Maine, with added notes on fecundity. *J. Mammal.* 32: 267-280.

Richardson, L. W., H. A. Jacobson, R. J. Muncy, and C. J. Perkins. 1983. Acoustics of white-tailed deer (*Odocoileus virginianus*). *J. Mammal.* 64: 245-252.

Robbins, C. T., and A. N. Moen. 1975. Milk composition and weight gain of white-tailed deer. *J. Wildlife Mgmt.* 39: 355-360.

Rogers, L. L., J. J. Mooty, and D. Dawson. 1981. *Foods of white-tailed deer in the Upper Great Lakes Region — a review.* USDA Forest Service General, Technical Report NC-65. USDA Forest Service, St. Paul, MN. 24 pp.

Samuel, W. M., and W. C. Glazener. 1970. Movement of white-tailed deer fawns in south Texas. *J. Wildlife Mgmt.* 34: 959-961.

Sauer, P. R., J. E. Tanck, and C. W. Severinghaus. 1969. Herbaceous food preferences of white-tailed deer. *N. Y. Fish and Game J.* 16:145-147.

Severinghaus, C. W. 1949. The willingness of nursing deer to adopt strange fawns. *J. Mammal.* 30: 75-76.

Short, H. L. 1975. Nutrition of southern deer in different seasons. *J. Wildlife Mgmt.* 321-329.

Silver, H. 1961. Deer milk compared with substitute milk for fawns. *J. Wildlife Mgmt.* 25:66-70.

Skinner, M. R., and E. S. Telfer. 1974. Spring, summer, and fall foods of deer in New Brunswick. *J. Wildlife Mgmt.* 38: 210-214.

Townsend, T. W., and E. D. Bailey. 1975. Parturitional, early maternal, and neonatal behavior in penned white-tailed deer. *J. Mammal.* 56: 347-362.

Vangilder, L. D., O. Torgerson, and W. R. Porth. 1982. Factors influencing diet selection by white-tailed deer. *J. Wildlife Mgmt.* 46: 711-718.

Verme, L. J. 1962. Mortality of white-tailed deer fawns. Proc. Nat. White-tailed Deer Dis. Symp. 1: 15-38.

Verme, L. J. 1963. Effect of nutrition on growth of white-tailed deer fawns. Trans. N. Amer. Wildl. and Natur. Resour. Conf. 28: 431-443.

Verme, L. J. 1969. Reproductive patterns of white-tailed deer related to nutritional plane. *J. Wildlife Mgmt.* 33: 881-887.

Verme, L. J. 1977. Assessment of natal mortality in Upper Michigan deer. *J. Wildlife Mgmt.* 41: 700-708.

Verme, L. J. 1979. Influence of nutrition on fetal organ development in deer. *J. Wildlife Mgmt.* 43: 791-796.

Verme, L. J., and J. J. Ozoga. 1981. Appraisal of autumn-spring weather severity for northern deer. *Wildl. Soc. Bull.* 9: 292-295.

Weckerly, F. W. 1992. Territoriality in North American deer: a call for a common definition. *Wildl. Soc. Bull.* 20: 228-231.

Weeks, H. P., and C. M. Kirkpatrick. 1976. Adaptations of white-tailed deer to naturally occurring sodium deficiencies. *J. Wildlife Mgmt.* 40: 610-625.

White, M. 1973. Description of remains of deer fawns killed by coyotes. *J. Mammal.* 54: 291-293.

White, M., F. F. Knowlton, and W. C. Glazener. 1972. Effects of dam-newborn fawn behavior on capture and mortality. *J. Wildlife Mgmt.* 36: 897-906.

Youatt, W. G., L. J. Verme, and D. E. Ullrey. 1965. Composition of milk and blood in nursing white-tailed deer does and blood composition of their fawns. *J. Wildlife Mgmt.* 29: 79-84.